Team Leaders Toolbox

Earn Trust, Motivate People, and Lead with Confidence

Stephen J. McIntyre

Echo Enterprise
An Imprint of Echo Story Media LLC

First published in 2025.

Cover and interior design by Stephen J. McIntyre.
Published by Echo Story Media LLC

ECHO
STORY
MEDIA

Echo Story Media LLC
30 N Gould St Ste R
Sheridan, WY 82801

ISBN: 979-8-9998500-2-7 (paperback)

For permissions requests, speaking inquiries, and bulk order purchase options, email info@echostorymedia.com or use our contact page https://echostorymedia.com/contact.

Disclaimer

This is a work of fiction. Names, characters, businesses, brands, places, events, locales, and incidents are either the product of the author's imagination or used in a fictitious manner. Any resemblance to actual persons, living or dead, or actual events is purely coincidental.

All product names, logos, brands, and other trademarks mentioned are the property of their respective trademark holders. Their use in this book is for descriptive purposes only and does not imply any affiliation with or endorsement by them.

Dedication

To Jaime, my partner in everything, and Harper, my brightest light. Thank you for letting me disappear into my writing without ever making me feel far away.

Table of Contents

Introduction

When I was first asked to lead a team, I did what most technically capable people do: I treated it like another problem to solve. I looked for logic in the noise, expected everyone to behave predictably, and tried to "optimise" how people worked. It didn't go how I imagined.

Leadership isn't like debugging code or refining a workflow. It's messy, emotional, human. Often, the real challenge isn't knowing what to do - it's knowing how to *be*. How to build trust, hold space for others, stay calm under pressure, and show up in a way that makes people want to follow you.

I started writing this book in 2010. Over the years, I rewrote it several times. At one point, I broke it into smaller how-to books. I tried frameworks, diagrams, leadership lists. They were all useful, but they weren't memorable. They didn't *stick*. Eventually, I realised that story is what stays with us. We remember the characters, the conversations, the moments of challenge and growth. That's how we learn.

Team Leaders Toolbox is a business parable. It follows Marcia Hughes, a newly promoted team leader thrust into a high-stakes environment with no formal leadership training. You'll walk with her through messy meetings, difficult conversations, moments of doubt, and key breakthroughs. Along the way, you'll pick up tools and principles that you can use in your own team - because the story is built around real situations I've seen play out in companies again and again.

If you're a first-time team leader, or even an experienced one looking for a fresh perspective, this book is for you. Whether you're leading in tech, consulting, operations, or any fast-moving field, the challenges are often the same: earning trust, aligning people, and making progress without burning out.

This book is designed to help you do three things:

1. **Recognise yourself** in the story.
2. **Reflect** on how you lead (or want to lead).
3. **Apply** practical ideas immediately in your work.

If you'd like to go further, I've included a collection of tools and templates in the Resources section. You'll find a Team Goals Framework, Skills Matrix Template, and more - all designed to support the concepts in the book.

Thanks for picking up this book. Let's begin.

Stephen J. McIntyre
Auckland, New Zealand

Chapter 1
The Promotion

Effective immediately, Marcia Hughes will assume the role of Team Leader for the Enterprise Solutions Development team.

Marcia read the email for a third time, her coffee cooling, forgotten beside her keyboard. The words didn't change, though their meaning refused to fully register. Her mouse pointer hovered over the message, as if clicking somewhere - anywhere - might reveal the actual intended recipient.

She pushed away from her desk, chair wheels gliding across worn carpet, and grabbed the spiral notebook she'd been using for debugging code. As Seattle's perpetual drizzle painted watercolour streaks down her window, she flipped past pages of system diagrams and error notes to a blank page. At the top, she wrote "Team leader?" with a question mark that felt heavier than the words themselves.

This notebook had been her companion through every technical challenge - her debugging log, her problem-solving space. Now it would have to become something else. Something she didn't quite have a name for yet.

The familiar symphony of office life continued around her - keyboards clicking, and conversations two desks away you couldn't not hear - while Marcia's brain short-circuited on two impossible words: *Team Leader.*

Team Leader? Her?

For three years at Alpha Consulting, she'd been the fixer, the problem-solver, the code whisperer. She'd built a reputation as someone who could tackle the thorniest technical problems, the developer they called when systems mysteriously crashed at midnight. What she hadn't done was lead anyone besides herself.

A knock on her cubicle wall interrupted her thoughts. James Anderson, VP of Development, stood there with a knowing smile. In his late forties with salt-and-pepper hair and the calm demeanour of someone who'd seen everything twice, James had always been supportive of Marcia's technical growth.

"I see you got the email," he said.

"I did," Marcia replied, gesturing vaguely at her screen. "Is this... I mean, was there a mistake? I didn't apply for a leadership position."

James chuckled, pulling up a spare chair. "No mistake. We need someone to lead the Enterprise Solutions team, and you're the right person for the job."

Marcia's scepticism must have shown on her face because James continued, "Look, I know this is unexpected. But Carl's departure for that startup left us in a tough spot. The FreshWorks client project is heating up, and the team needs someone who understands the technical challenges inside and out."

"But managing people isn't the same as managing code," Marcia protested. "I debug systems. People are... messier."

"True," James nodded, "but systems don't build themselves. People do. And those people need someone who understands both the technical and human elements."

Marcia fidgeted with a pen on her desk. "The team already has Victor with his ten years of experience. Or Mei, who seems to get along with everyone. Why not them?"

"Victor is brilliant technically but struggles with change and communication. Mei connects well with people but second-guesses her technical decisions. The team needs someone with your combination of technical clarity and practical problem-solving. Someone who can see where we need to go."

Marcia felt a flutter of panic. "I don't know the first thing about being a team leader."

James smiled. "Nobody does at first. I certainly didn't when I started." He leaned forward. "Let me ask you this - when you're solving a complex technical problem, what's your approach?"

"I break it down into manageable components," Marcia answered automatically. "Isolate variables, create a structured plan, implement step by step, measure results, adjust."

"Exactly," James nodded. "Leadership responds to the same approach. The variables are just different. Instead of code modules, you're working with people's skills, motivations, and communication styles."

Marcia wasn't convinced, but something in James's confidence was reassuring. "What if I mess it up? The FreshWorks project is critical."

James let the question hang for a full heartbeat, the office hum filling the silence. "You probably will mess some things up," James said at last with unexpected candour. "Everyone does. But you'll learn fast. And I'll be here to help."

He stood up, straightening his jacket. "The team meeting is at 2 pm in Conference Room C. That's your first opportunity to step into the role. I'll be there to announce the change, but then it's your show."

Marcia's fingers tightened around the edge of her desk. She was already rehearsing how she might sound in the team meeting - calm, collected, authoritative. But inside, a wave of self-doubt kept rising. Was she just going to fake her way through this and hope no one noticed? Maybe that's what leadership looked like - pretending you belonged until it became true.

As James turned to leave, Marcia called after him. "Wait! What exactly am I supposed to do with them?"

James paused. "Start by listening. Really listening. Understand their strengths, concerns, what they need to succeed. Then build from there." He tapped his watch. "You've got three hours to prepare. Use them wisely."

After he left, Marcia sat motionless for several minutes, her mind racing. She'd never considered management as part of her career path. She took pride in being the problem-solver, the technical guru others came to for help. Now she was supposed to be responsible for an entire team's performance?

She exhaled. Too loud. Too shaky. Was she ready? God, what if they found out she wasn't? The familiar weight of impostor syndrome settled on her shoulders like a heavy coat. She'd felt this before - in her first technical presentation to senior management, when she'd stammered through slides about database optimisation while her hands trembled. That time, she'd recovered by diving deep into the data, letting the numbers speak for her. But people weren't numbers. You couldn't debug a team the way you debugged code.

Marcia straightened her shoulders, forcing herself to breathe normally. Maybe she wasn't ready. Maybe she'd never feel ready. But James believed in her, and right now, that would have to be enough.

With a deep breath, Marcia opened a new document on her computer and titled it "Team Leader Approach." Her fingers hovered over the keyboard. What did she actually know about the Enterprise Solutions team members? She'd worked with them occasionally but never paid much attention to how they operated as a group.

She began typing notes, organising what little information she had:

Victor Kowalski:
Senior developer, South African, brilliant with databases, particular about his work environment, doesn't handle interruptions well.

Mei Lin:
Mid-level developer, friendly, brings snacks to share, good at defusing tensions, sometimes hesitates on technical decisions.

Dmitri Petrov:
Database specialist, quiet, precise, keeps to himself.

Plus, two other developers she barely knew.

It wasn't much to go on. How was she supposed to lead people she barely understood?

Marcia pushed back from her desk again and stood up. Before overthinking this further, she needed more information. She decided to walk through the office and observe the team in their natural habitat before the official meeting.

As she gathered her things, her computer pinged with another email - this one from Elizabeth Parker, the executive contact at FreshWorks. The subject line read "Concerns About Project Timeline."

Perfect. Not only was she now responsible for a team she barely knew, but their most important client was already unhappy. Marcia took a deep breath and clicked on the email.

She just hoped people could be debugged as easily as code.

✦　✦　✦

Marcia walked through Alpha Consulting's open office space, notebook in hand. At just ten years old, the company had grown from a scrappy startup to a respectable mid-sized consulting firm, though the office still had that slightly worn, practical feel of a company that prioritised client results over aesthetics.

As she approached the Enterprise Solutions area, she slowed her pace and observed. The team occupied a cluster of cubicles near the windows, their grey fabric walls adorned with various personal touches. Most desks featured standard company-issued laptops connected to the corporate network through ethernet cables - only Victor had managed to convince IT to grant him two extra monitors, a privilege typically reserved for senior designers and executives.

Unlike her own meticulously organised workspace, each team member's area reflected distinct personalities. The shared printer in the corner was surrounded by stacks of documentation and requirement specifications printed for review, as the team still relied heavily on physical documents despite the company's recent SharePoint implementation that many were reluctant to fully adopt.

Victor's desk was a fortress of precisely arranged monitors and reference materials. Three screens displayed database schemas, and sticky notes formed a color-coded system along his cubicle wall. He sat with noise-cancelling headphones, fingers flying across his keyboard, completely unaware of her presence.

A few desks over, Mei Lin's workspace burst with colour - family photos, small plants, and a jar of candy sat alongside her computer. She was on the phone, nodding enthusiastically while making notes, a friendly smile on her face even though the caller couldn't see it.

In the corner, Dmitri hunched over his keyboard, his desk spartan except for a small Russian flag. His cubicle walls were bare, his desktop clear of anything but essential tools. He glanced up briefly as Marcia passed, giving a curt nod before returning to his work.

The other two developers - Jason and Priya, if she remembered correctly - were away from their desks.

Marcia hesitated, suddenly feeling like an intruder. These people had been working together under Carl's leadership for months, maybe years. Now she was supposed to step in and take over?

She was about to retreat when Mei spotted her and waved her over.

"Marcia! Hello!" Mei hung up her phone. "What brings you to our little neighbourhood? Another integration emergency?"

"Actually, I..." Marcia began, then realised she wasn't sure if she should announce her new role before the official meeting. "I was hoping to chat about the FreshWorks project. I'm getting more involved."

"Oh?" Mei's eyebrows rose in interest. "That's great! We could use the help. Since Carl left, things have been a bit..." she lowered her voice, "chaotic."

Victor, apparently sensing conversation, removed one side of his headphones without turning around. "If you're talking about the FreshWorks API issues, I've documented the authentication problems in the shared drive. The client's security requirements keep changing, which is creating cascading issues across the system."

Marcia approached his desk. "Actually, Victor, I was hoping to understand the overall project status before the team meeting later."

Victor turned now, his expression guarded. "Team meeting? There's nothing on my calendar."

"James just scheduled it for 2 pm," Marcia explained. "I thought everyone knew."

"First I'm hearing of it," Victor muttered, immediately checking his calendar. "I had planned to complete the database migration script this afternoon. This disrupts my flow."

Mei appeared at Victor's cubicle. "I got the invitation just a few minutes ago. I was going to remind everyone." She gave Marcia an apologetic smile. "Victor prefers advance notice for meetings."

"I prefer not having unnecessary meetings at all," Victor corrected. "We lost our team lead and haven't received a replacement. Meanwhile, Elizabeth Parker keeps emailing about timeline concerns without understanding the technical challenges. Another meeting won't solve these problems."

Marcia felt a knot forming in her stomach. "I actually just saw an email from Elizabeth. What exactly is she concerned about?"

Victor sighed heavily. "The client's leadership promised features we advised against implementing in this phase. Now they're upset about delays they created through their own requirement changes."

"That's not entirely fair," came a voice from behind them. Dmitri had silently approached. "The authentication issues were identified in initial planning. We should have anticipated the complications."

Victor's face hardened. "If I had been consulted during the planning phase - "

"You were on vacation," Dmitri interrupted, his accent becoming more pronounced as his voice tensed. "Some of us had to make decisions while you were taking three weeks in Cape Town."

Mei stepped between them with practiced ease. "Let's save this for the meeting, shall we? Marcia's just trying to get up to speed.". Mei had already connected the dots.

An uncomfortable silence fell over the group. Marcia frantically tried to think of something to say that wouldn't make things worse.

"I understand everyone's frustrated," she began carefully. "The project has clearly hit some rough patches. I'm hoping to help smooth things out."

"Unless you can add more hours to the day or developers to the team, I'm not sure how," Victor muttered, turning back to his screens.

Marcia felt her confidence wavering. This team was more fractured than she'd realised. How was she supposed to lead people who couldn't even agree on the nature of their problems?

Just then, Jason and Priya returned, deep in conversation about what sounded like a testing framework. They stopped abruptly when they noticed the small gathering.

"Did we miss something?" Jason asked, adjusting his glasses.

"Just discussing the FreshWorks project," Mei explained lightly. "Marcia was asking about the status."

"Oh," Priya looked surprised. "Are you joining the team, Marcia?"

Before she could answer, James appeared at the entrance to the team area.

"I see you're getting a head start," he said to Marcia with an approving nod. "Good. I'm looking forward to our meeting at 2." He addressed the team. "Everyone, make sure you're there. Important announcements to discuss."

As James walked away, five pairs of eyes turned to Marcia with varying degrees of curiosity and suspicion.

"What announcement?" Victor asked directly.

Marcia took a deep breath. This wasn't how she'd planned to begin, but there was no avoiding it now.

"I think James wants to share that himself," she said diplomatically. "But it appears I'll be working more closely with all of you on the FreshWorks project going forward."

Mei smiled encouragingly, while Dmitri gave a noncommittal shrug. Victor turned back to his monitors without comment. Jason and Priya exchanged glances that Marcia couldn't read.

"Guess we'll get the details at 2," Jason said, breaking the tension.

Marcia nodded and backed away. "Looking forward to it," she said, trying to sound more confident than she felt.

As she walked back to her desk, Marcia's mind raced. In less than fifteen minutes of interaction, she'd witnessed territorial disputes, communication breakdowns, and simmering resentments. And these were the people she was supposed to unify and lead?

She flipped open her notebook and added to her earlier notes:

Team seems fragmented. Technical disagreements. Communication issues. Need to address project concerns with Elizabeth Parker. Possible resistance to new leadership.

One thing was becoming clear - this leadership role would be far more challenging than debugging even the most complex code. And the team meeting at 2 pm was only the beginning of those challenges.

✧ ✧ ✧

Conference Room C was one of the smaller meeting spaces at Alpha Consulting - just large enough for eight people around an oval table. Marcia arrived fifteen minutes early, arranging her notes and connecting her laptop to the projector. The room felt stuffy, so she cracked open a window, letting in the gentle patter of Seattle's drizzle.

At 1:58 pm, James arrived with a reassuring nod. "Ready?"

Marcia inhaled, smoothed the waiver from her voice, and replied, "As I'll ever be."

The team filtered in over the next few minutes. Victor entered first, precisely at 2:00 pm, claiming a seat as far from the window as possible and immediately setting up his laptop and a stack of sticky notes. Mei followed, carrying a small container of homemade cookies that she placed in the centre of the table with an encouraging smile toward Marcia. Dmitri slipped in quietly, taking a seat at the far end. Jason and Priya entered together, still discussing what sounded like a technical disagreement in hushed tones.

The final person to enter was unfamiliar to Marcia - a slender man in his early thirties with a tablet under his arm.

"Thomas Nguyen," James explained, noticing Marcia's questioning look. "Quality Analyst recently assigned to the team."

Thomas gave a small wave as he took the last available seat.

James cleared his throat once everyone was settled. "Thank you all for being here. As you know, Carl's departure has left us with a leadership gap at a critical time for the FreshWorks project." He gestured toward Marcia. "I'm pleased to announce that Marcia Hughes will be stepping into the Team Leader role, effective immediately."

The room fell silent. Marcia felt six pairs of eyes evaluating her with varying degrees of surprise, curiosity, and in Victor's case, what looked suspiciously like disapproval.

"Marcia has demonstrated exceptional technical ability during her time with us," James continued. "Her problem-solving skills and attention to detail make her the ideal person to lead this team through the current challenges and beyond."

Mei was the first to respond with a warm, "Congratulations, Marcia!"

"Thanks," Marcia said, trying to project confidence she didn't feel. "I'm... looking forward to working with all of you more closely." she said, her voice steady but just a beat too late, like she was catching up to the words as she spoke them.

James turned to her. "I'll let you take it from here. I'll check in with you later." With an encouraging pat on her shoulder, he left the room, closing the door behind him.

The silence that followed felt heavier than before.

"So," Victor finally spoke, "you're our new leader. No disrespect, but what leadership experience do you have?"

Marcia had anticipated this question. "I haven't formally led a team before," she admitted. "But I've managed complex technical projects and coordinated cross-functional work throughout my career."

"Technical skills and leadership skills aren't the same thing," Victor pressed.

"You're right," Marcia acknowledged. "They're not. But I believe good leadership starts with understanding the work, the challenges, and most importantly, the people doing that work. That's why I wanted this meeting - to understand where we are and how I can help."

Dmitri folded his arms. "We are behind schedule with no clear path to meet the client's expectations. That is where we are."

"Elizabeth Parker emailed me this morning with concerns," Marcia said. "Can someone break down exactly what we've promised versus what we can deliver?"

For the next ten minutes, the team painted a grim picture. The FreshWorks project - a custom enterprise solution for a rapidly growing retail chain - was six weeks into development with another eight to go before the promised delivery date. Requirements had shifted multiple times, particularly around user authentication and reporting features. Carl's abrupt departure had left several critical decisions unmade.

"The main issue," Priya explained, "is that we're working from different understanding of priorities. I'm focused on the inventory module because that's what Carl emphasised last month, but now Elizabeth is asking about the reporting features."

"Which were supposed to be Phase Two," Victor added. "But apparently someone promised them for the initial release."

Thomas, who had been quiet until now, spoke up. "From a QA perspective, we don't even have testable builds for the core functionality yet. I've been testing fragments, but I can't verify end-to-end workflows."

Marcia jotted notes rapidly, trying to map the disconnected pieces into a coherent picture. "What about the authentication issues Victor mentioned earlier?"

This triggered a heated exchange between Victor and Dmitri about the best approach to handling the client's complex security requirements. Their technical disagreement quickly devolved into thinly veiled personal criticism.

"If we had followed standard security protocols from the beginning - " Victor started.

"Your 'standard protocols' would have added three weeks to the timeline," Dmitri cut in.

"And now we're spending four weeks fixing the shortcut approach," Victor shot back.

Mei tried to mediate. "Both approaches had merits - "

"There's no merit in doing something wrong just because it's faster," Victor snapped.

Marcia watched as the conversation spiralled, team members talking over each other, old grievances surfacing. Jason and Priya had stopped contributing entirely, while Thomas looked increasingly uncomfortable. This wasn't just a project with challenges - it was a team in disarray.

"Okay, everyone, let's take a step back," Marcia finally interjected, raising her voice slightly to cut through the crosstalk. The room quieted, though tension still crackled in the air.

Victor flinched at the sudden hush, fingers drumming his laptop in a frantic staccato before he compulsively realigned his stack of colour-coded sticky notes perfectly parallel to his laptop.

"First, thank you for being candid," she said. "It's clear we have significant technical and communication challenges to address."

She turned to the whiteboard and picked up a marker. "If - uh, if we just group what I'm hearing into categories, maybe we can see where the bottlenecks are - like, um, *technical*," pausing as she wrote. "*Resource* " she fixed the last e by shortening the tail with her finger, "*gaps*, ". Feeling slightly flustered because spelling was always harder with people watching, she finished "And, uh, *cli-ent ex-pec-ta-tions*?" she sounded out to help spell it.

There were reluctant nods around the table.

"Good. Now before we dive deeper into solutions, I'd like to understand something fundamental. What does success look like for each of you on this project? Not just delivering features, but what would make you feel this project was worthwhile?"

The question seemed to catch everyone off guard.

After a moment, Mei spoke first. "Personally, I'd like us to deliver something that genuinely helps FreshWorks' employees. They're struggling with their current systems."

"I want to implement the authentication framework properly," Victor said. "Current approach is technically flawed."

"Meeting our commitments to the client," Dmitri stated flatly.

Thomas added, "Delivering quality software without last-minute panic fixes."

As each person shared their perspective, Marcia noticed something important - they all had different visions of success, different priorities. No wonder they were pulling in different directions.

"Thank you for sharing that," she said when everyone had spoken. "I'm hearing different but complementary goals. To succeed, we need to align these perspectives into a unified approach."

She turned back to the whiteboard and began sketching a basic project timeline. "For our next meeting, I'd like each of you to prepare two things: first, a candid assessment of your current tasks and their status; second, what you need from others to be successful."

Victor raised his hand slightly. "And what about the immediate authentication issues? We need decisions now, not in the next meeting."

Marcia nodded. "You're right. Let's schedule a technical discussion for Monday morning - you, Dmitri, and me. We'll resolve the approach then."

As she continued outlining next steps, Marcia noticed the team's expressions shifting. The open hostility had faded, replaced by cautious attention. They weren't convinced yet, but at least they were listening.

The meeting wrapped up after forty-five minutes, with specific action items assigned to each person. As the team filed out, Mei lingered behind.

"That was... interesting," she said with a small smile. "I haven't seen Victor and Dmitri in the same room without arguing in weeks."

"They still argued," Marcia pointed out.

"Yes, but you redirected it. That's more than Carl managed toward the end." Mei pushed the container of cookies toward her. "Take one. You earned it."

After Mei left, Marcia sank back into her chair, exhaling slowly. The meeting had been even more challenging than she'd anticipated. The team wasn't just lacking leadership - they were fractured, with competing priorities and communication styles that clashed spectacularly.

She pulled out her notebook and wrote:

Need unified team goals. Clarify individual roles. Establish communication protocols. Address technical disagreements directly.

While she collected her things to leave, her phone buzzed with an email notification. Elizabeth Parker again: *Looking forward to our status call Monday. Need assurances on timeline.*

Marcia closed her eyes briefly. She had less than one working day to get a handle on the technical issues, prepare for a client call, and somehow begin transforming this group of talented but misaligned individuals into an actual team.

She needed help, and she knew exactly who to ask. James had offered his support, and it was time to take him up on it. She needed to understand not just the technical aspects of leadership, but how to navigate the human complexities that no debugging tool could solve.

✧ ✧ ✧

The Seattle skyline was fading into twilight as Marcia knocked on James's office door. Through the glass, she could see him on the phone, but he waved her in with a smile. His office was modest but thoughtfully arranged bookshelves lined one wall, while framed photos of mountain climbing expeditions decorated another. A large whiteboard covered with project timelines dominated the third wall.

James wrapped up his call. "Elizabeth Parker?" Marcia asked as he hung up.

"How did you guess?" He gestured to the chair across from his desk. "She's understandably concerned about the project."

"Join the club," Marcia sighed, dropping into the chair. "I finished the team meeting, and..." she trailed off, searching for the right words.

"That bad?" James asked, leaning forward.

"Worse." Marcia ran a hand through her dark hair. "James, this isn't just a team without a leader. It's barely a team at all. They're like separate planets orbiting different suns."

James nodded thoughtfully. "Tell me what you observed."

Marcia spent the next few minutes detailing the meeting - Victor's territorial stance on the authentication system, Dmitri's competing approach, the confusion about priorities, Thomas's concerns about testing, and the general lack of coordination.

"I tried to establish some structure for moving forward," she concluded, "but on Monday I have to referee a technical dispute and somehow reassure Elizabeth that we're on track - when we're clearly not."

James leaned back in his chair. "Welcome to leadership," he said with a wry smile. "Where the problems are always more complex than they first appear."

"This isn't what I signed up for," Marcia admitted. "I solve technical problems. These are people problems."

"Are they, though?" James asked. "Or are they system problems that manifest through people?"

Marcia considered this. "What do you mean?"

James stood and walked to his whiteboard, erasing a section. "Let me share something I learned during my military service." He drew a simple diagram with three interconnected circles. "In any team environment, there are three key elements: the task, the process, and the people." He labelled each circle accordingly.

"Most new leaders," he continued, "focus exclusively on the task - what needs to be done. But tasks don't exist in isolation." He tapped the 'process' circle. "How the work gets done is equally important." Then he touched the 'people' circle. "And who is doing it - with their unique skills, motivations, and communication styles - completes the picture."

Marcia leaned forward, intrigued despite her exhaustion. "So, you're saying I need to address all three?"

"I'm saying they're interconnected. When a team is struggling, the issue rarely lies in just one area." James capped his marker. "The symptoms might look like people problems - Victor and Dmitri arguing, for instance. But the root cause could be unclear processes for making technical decisions, or misaligned understanding of the task priorities."

"That makes sense," Marcia acknowledged. "But how do I even begin untangling all this?"

James returned to his seat. "You're already starting the right way - by observing before acting. Most leaders rush to impose solutions before they understand the real problems."

He pulled a folder from his desk drawer and handed it to Marcia. "Here's something that might help. A framework I've used with teams in transition."

The folder contained several documents, the top one titled Team Leaders Toolbox. Marcia flipped through the pages, seeing sections on team goals, skills matrix, resource allocation, and roadmap planning.

"This is a systematic approach to building team alignment," James explained. "It starts with establishing clear goals - not just what the team needs to deliver, but how they'll work together."

"Like a team charter?" Marcia asked.

"More fundamental than that. It's about getting everyone oriented in the same direction first. Once you have that foundation, you can address the more specific issues."

Marcia nodded slowly, continuing to browse the document. "This is more structured than I expected."

"You're an engineer, Marcia. You appreciate systems and structures. Why not apply that same systematic thinking to leadership?" James smiled. "Don't try to become a different person overnight. Use your analytical strengths as a foundation for your leadership approach."

For the first time since receiving the promotion email that morning, Marcia felt a glimmer of confidence. This was something she could work with - a framework, a system, a logical approach to a complex problem.

"Before you dive in," James cautioned, "there's something important to understand. Leading isn't the same as managing. Management is about controlling and directing. Leadership is about creating the conditions where people can do their best work."

"What's the difference in practice?" Marcia asked.

"Observation," James replied simply. "Watch before you act. Learn how your team members work best. What motivates them. What frustrates them. What skills they have that aren't being fully utilised."

He leaned forward, his expression serious. "Monday, when you meet with Victor and Dmitri, resist the urge to jump to a technical solution yourself. Instead, guide them toward finding common ground. When you talk to Elizabeth, don't make promises you can't keep - focus on establishing a process for getting to realistic commitments."

Marcia nodded. "Observe, then act. I can do that." She tapped the folder. "And this will give me a framework to follow."

"Exactly." James glanced at his watch. "It's getting late. Review those materials over the weekend if you can, but don't overwhelm yourself. This is a marathon, not a sprint."

As Marcia gathered her things to leave, James added, "One more thing. Leadership isn't about having all the answers. It's about asking the right questions and creating space for your team to find the answers together."

"That's not exactly comforting when I have Elizabeth expecting answers on Monday," Marcia pointed out.

James chuckled. "Fair point. But remember - you don't need to solve everything at once. Focus on establishing a clear process for getting to solutions. That's often more valuable than the solutions themselves."

Walking back to her desk to collect her laptop, Marcia's mind was already processing the conversation with James. The three-circle model made sense - task, process, people. She'd been so focused on the technical aspects (the task) that she hadn't considered how the work was being done (the process) or who was doing it (the people).

She glanced at the Enterprise Solutions team area, now empty as everyone had gone home for the day. Monday would bring the technical meeting with Victor and Dmitri, followed by the client call with Elizabeth. Both would be challenging, but now she had at least the beginnings of an approach.

As she shouldered her bag, Marcia realised something important. The problem wasn't just that the team lacked leadership - they lacked a shared understanding of what they were trying to accomplish together. Before she could address the technical disagreements or reassure the client, she needed to help the team find common ground.

The Team Leaders Toolbox materials tucked under her arm felt like a lifeline. She wasn't starting from scratch after all. She had a framework to build on, a systematic approach that aligned with her natural problem-solving instincts.

Still, the quiet voice hadn't gone away - the one that whispered she wasn't ready, that she was about to be exposed.

She'd learned to drown it in strategy, in structure, in over-preparedness. Maybe this time would be no different.

At the same time, she felt an increasing sense of possibility. Maybe she could do this after all - not by becoming someone else, but by applying her existing strengths in a new context.

The rain had intensified as she headed to the parking garage, Seattle's evening commute in full swing. Monday would be a test, but at least now she had a map to guide her through the unfamiliar terrain of leadership.

Chapter 2
Differing Perspectives

Marcia arrived at the office early on Monday morning, clutching a large coffee and the folder James had given her. She'd spent time over the weekend reviewing the materials, particularly the section on understanding team dynamics. One passage had stuck with her: "Each team member has unique needs, working styles, and motivations. A leader's job is to understand these differences, not eliminate them."

With that in mind, she'd decided to meet individually with Victor before the larger technical discussion. Based on Friday's interactions, he seemed to be both the most technically knowledgeable and the most resistant to her leadership.

The office was mostly empty at 7:30 am, but as she'd suspected, Victor was already at his desk, headphones on, fingers darting across his keyboard. His workspace looked even more organised in the morning light - reference books arranged by height, pens lined up by colour, monitors positioned at precise angles.

Marcia approached and waited at the edge of his cubicle until he noticed her. Victor startled slightly, then removed his headphones.

"Morning," she said. "Do you have a few minutes to talk before our meeting with Dmitri?"

Victor glanced at his monitor, clearly reluctant to break his concentration. "Is it necessary? I'm in the middle of refactoring the authentication module."

"I think it could help us have a more productive discussion later," Marcia replied. "I'd like to understand your perspective better."

After a moment's hesitation, Victor nodded, his hands briefly stilling on the table. At his stage of career, every process change felt like an implicit criticism of methods that had served him well for decades. But Marcia was asking for his expertise, not dismissing it - a distinction that mattered more than he cared to admit. "Twenty minutes," he said, checking his watch. "I have a code review at 8:30 am."

"Perfect. Let's use the small meeting room."

As they walked, Marcia noticed how Victor straightened the chairs they passed and adjusted a crooked picture frame on the wall. In the meeting room, he immediately realigned the chairs to be equidistant from the table.

Once they were seated, Marcia decided to be direct. "Victor, I get the sense you have concerns about my leading this team."

His expression remained neutral. "I have concerns about anyone leading this team without a clear understanding of the technical complexities we're facing."

"That's fair," Marcia acknowledged. "Which is why I wanted to talk with you first. You have the most experience with the authentication system, and I need to understand it better."

Victor seemed surprised by this approach. After a moment, he reached for the whiteboard marker. "May I?"

For the next ten minutes, Victor outlined the authentication system with remarkable clarity, diagramming components and explaining decision points. Marcia asked questions intermittently, taking notes. As he explained, she noticed how his entire demeanour changed - his movements became fluid, his speech more confident, his eyes bright with engagement.

"So the core issue," Victor concluded, "is that Dmitri's approach prioritises speed over scalability. It works now, but will create significant problems when the client adds international locations next year."

"What would your approach entail?" Marcia asked.

"Three additional days of development now to implement proper federated authentication. It would delay the current sprint but prevent a complete rewrite later." Victor put down the marker and looked at her expectantly.

Instead of responding directly, Marcia tried a different angle. "How would you prioritise this against the other technical challenges we're facing?"

Victor blinked, seemingly thrown by the question. "I... haven't considered that," he admitted.

"What would help you work most effectively on this problem?" Marcia continued.

Victor thought for a moment. "Uninterrupted time. Clear specifications. And..." he hesitated, "not having my approach dismissed without technical consideration."

Marcia nodded. "That makes sense. And has that been happening?"

"Carl would often side with whoever spoke most convincingly, not who had the strongest technical argument," Victor said stiffly. "It was... frustrating."

"I can imagine," Marcia said. "I appreciate technical rigor too."

Victor studied her, his expression softening slightly. "You built the inventory integration system last year, didn't you? The one that automated the reconciliation process?"

Marcia nodded, surprised he knew about her work.

"That was elegant code," Victor said, offering what felt like his highest compliment. "I reviewed it when we were planning a similar approach for FreshWorks."

"Thank you," Marcia said, genuinely touched. "I'm still proud of that solution."

Victor glanced at his watch. "Our twenty minutes are nearly up."

"Just one more question," Marcia said. "In your ideal scenario, how would technical decisions be made on this team?"

Victor considered this carefully. "Based on architectural principles and technical merit, with adequate time for proper implementation." He paused, then added, "And with respect for specialised expertise."

Marcia nodded, making another note. "Thanks for being candid. This helps me understand your perspective better."

As they walked back toward the main office area, Victor stopped suddenly. "You didn't tell me what you're going to decide about the authentication system."

"I haven't decided yet," Marcia replied honestly. "I want to hear Dmitri's perspective first, and understand how this fits into our overall priorities."

Victor frowned slightly. "But you're the leader. Isn't it your job to make these decisions?"

"My job is to ensure we make the right decisions as a team," Marcia said. "Sometimes that means I decide directly. Other times it means creating a process for better decision-making."

Victor seemed to turn this over in his mind. "That's... different from what I expected."

Victor's posture relaxed almost imperceptibly. After thirty years in software development, he'd grown weary of defending approaches that had proven their worth, of explaining why precision mattered in a world that seemed to value speed over accuracy. But here was someone who actually wanted to understand his perspective rather than simply override it.

"Different good or different bad?" Marcia asked with a slight smile.

"Undetermined," Victor replied, but his tone was lighter than before. "I'll reserve judgment pending further data."

As Victor returned to his desk, Marcia felt cautiously optimistic. The conversation had revealed several important insights: Victor valued technical excellence and proper planning. He felt his expertise was often overlooked. And most importantly, he responded well to having his knowledge respected.

She jotted a few more notes in her notebook:

Victor: Needs structure, clear processes, recognition of expertise. Likely on autism spectrum? Prioritises technical correctness over deadlines. Strengths: detailed technical knowledge, systematic thinking. Explain "why" behind decisions.

Glancing at her watch, Marcia realised it was nearly time for the technical meeting with both Victor and Dmitri. This conversation had been a promising start, but navigating between their competing approaches would be the real test. Victor clearly had strong technical opinions - but what drove Dmitri's perspective? She needed to understand his viewpoint just as thoroughly.

As she pulled together her notes, Marcia spotted Dmitri arriving at his desk, his expression characteristically serious. Understanding Victor better was just the first step in a more complex process of bringing this fragmented team together. The technical disagreement over authentication was just a symptom of deeper misalignment. Addressing the immediate issue was necessary, but she was beginning to see that building a cohesive team would require much more than resolving individual disputes.

✦ ✦ ✦

By mid-morning, the FreshWorks authentication issue had been temporarily resolved. The meeting with Victor and Dmitri had gone better than expected - Marcia had focused on establishing clear decision criteria rather than imposing a solution, which seemed to satisfy both developers. They'd agreed to implement Victor's more robust approach but with a phased timeline that addressed Dmitri's concerns about immediate deliverables.

Now Marcia sat at her desk, reviewing Elizabeth Parker's latest email about project milestones. The client call was scheduled for 2 pm, giving her a few hours to get a better understanding of the team's overall progress. She needed to speak with each team member, starting with Dmitri.

Unlike Victor's meticulous workspace, Dmitri's desk offered few clues about his personality. No photos, minimal decorations - just his small flag and a few carefully placed technical books. She'd noticed during the morning meeting that while Victor was vocal and assertive, Dmitri spoke only when directly addressed, his responses precise but minimal.

Marcia approached his desk, where he was intently focused on his monitor.

"Dmitri, do you have a moment?"

He looked up, his expression neutral. "Yes." His single-word response hung in the air.

"I'd like to check in about your current tasks for the FreshWorks project. Maybe we could grab a coffee in the break room?"

Dmitri glanced at his screen, then back at Marcia. "I can spare fifteen minutes."

The break room was empty except for Jason, who was microwaving something that smelled strongly of curry. He nodded to them and returned to his phone - the latest iPhone that had sparked an ongoing debate in the office about whether it was better than the BlackBerry devices some managers still clung to. Jason stood scrolling through his Facebook feed as they settled at a small table in the corner.

"How are things going with the database integration?" Marcia asked, opening her notebook.

"It is progressing," Dmitri replied. "I should complete the core functionality by Friday."

"That's good to hear. Any obstacles I should know about?"

Dmitri hesitated, his fingers tapping lightly on the table - the first sign of nervousness Marcia had seen from him. "No significant obstacles."

His right hand trembled slightly as he reached for his coffee cup, and he steadied it against the table before continuing. The tremor was barely noticeable, but Marcia caught it - a small crack in his otherwise composed facade.

Marcia thought back to James's advice about observation. Something in Dmitri's hesitation suggested he wasn't sharing the full picture.

"I noticed in our team meeting Friday that you mentioned being behind schedule," she probed gently. "What's contributing to that?"

Dmitri's expression remained impassive, but his finger tapping increased slightly. His breathing had become shallow, and when he glanced toward Jason in the break room, there was something almost protective in the way he positioned himself - as if any additional scrutiny might shatter his carefully maintained composure. "The schedule was... optimistic from the beginning. Some features are taking longer than estimated."

"Whose estimates were they?"

"Carl made the final estimates for the client," Dmitri said. "After consulting with the team."

There was something in his tone - a slight emphasis on 'final' - that caught Marcia's attention.

"Were your original estimates different?" she asked.

Dmitri's eyes flicked briefly to Jason, who was still in the break room, before returning to Marcia. "My estimates were... adjusted to meet client expectations."

"Adjusted downward, I'm guessing?" Marcia said quietly.

A small nod was his only answer.

"By how much?"

Dmitri sighed almost imperceptibly. "For the database integration, I estimated three weeks. It was reduced to two in the project plan."

"And you agreed to this?"

"I was told to make it work," Dmitri replied, his voice utterly flat. "So, I am trying to make it work."

Marcia made some notes. "Are you working additional hours to try to meet this timeline?"

"Some evenings. Most weekends." He stated this as simple fact, without complaint.

"Since when?"

"Since the project began six weeks ago."

Marcia set down her pen. Six weeks of evenings and weekends would explain the fatigue she'd glimpsed behind his stoic expression.

"Why didn't you mention this during our meeting on Friday?"

Dmitri shrugged slightly. "It would not change the deadlines. The client expects what they were promised."

But then something shifted in his expression - barely perceptible, like clouds passing over a distant mountain. For just a moment, his carefully neutral mask slipped, and Marcia caught a glimpse of something raw underneath. He straightened his shoulders as if making a decision, then met her eyes directly for the first time in their conversation.

"Even if those promises were unrealistic?"

"Especially then," Dmitri replied with unexpected bitterness. "In my experience, admitting you cannot meet a deadline only creates... complications."

"What kind of complications?"

Dmitri was silent for a moment, choosing his words carefully. "In my previous position, those who could not meet deadlines were replaced with those who claimed they could." His eyes met hers directly for the first time. "Whether they actually delivered was less important than their willingness to say yes."

The pieces were starting to come together. Dmitri's reluctance to push back on unrealistic timelines, his stoic acceptance of impossible workloads, his silence when overloaded - all stemmed from professional survival instincts developed in a different environment.

"Dmitri, I need to be clear about something," Marcia said. "I'd rather hear honest bad news early than optimistic fiction that becomes a crisis later. I can't help with problems I don't know about."

His expression remained sceptical.

"Let me ask you directly," she continued. "With the current requirements and your available working hours - standard hours, not nights and weekends - when could you realistically deliver the database integration with the quality level we need?"

Dmitri considered the question carefully. "Three and a half weeks from the start. So, another week and a half from today."

"That's a week later than the current plan," Marcia noted.

"Yes," Dmitri acknowledged, tension visible in his shoulders as if expecting a negative reaction.

Instead, Marcia made another note. "Thank you for being honest. Now, are there any dependencies I should know about? Is anyone waiting on your work, or are you waiting on anyone else?"

"Thomas needs my components for testing. And I need final field specifications from Priya for three modules."

"Has Priya given you a timeline for those specs?"

"She said 'soon,'" Dmitri replied with a hint of frustration. "Two weeks ago."

"Why haven't you followed up?"

"She has her own deadlines. I did not want to..." he searched for the right phrase, "add to her burden."

Marcia was beginning to understand a critical dynamic. Dmitri was drowning in work but unwilling to create "complications" for others or admit he was struggling. Meanwhile, his silence was creating cascading delays that affected the entire team.

"One last question," Marcia said. "What would help you be most effective in your role right now?"

Dmitri seemed startled by the question. After a long pause, he answered, "Clear specifications. Realistic timelines." Another pause. "And knowing that raising concerns will not be seen as... failure."

As they stood to return to their desks, Marcia made a decision. "Dmitri, I'd like you to send me a detailed breakdown of your current tasks, with your genuine estimates for each. Not what you think I want to hear, but what you truly believe it will take."

His expression grew guarded. "And if those estimates exceed the client's expectations?"

"Then we adjust either the expectations or the approach," Marcia said firmly. "But we start with reality, not wishful thinking."

Dmitri studied her, as if trying to determine if she was serious. "I will send this by end of day," he finally said.

"Thank you," Marcia replied. "And Dmitri? This weekend, I want you to rest. No work. That's not a suggestion - it's a direction."

A flicker of something like relief crossed his face. For a moment, his shoulders dropped as if he'd been holding his breath for weeks. "My visa status..." he began quietly, then stopped. "There have been complications with my application. I did not want to seem unreliable when the company might need to make... decisions about my future." The admission hung between them, raw and vulnerable.

Back at her desk, Marcia added to her growing notes on team dynamics:

Dmitri: Reluctant to communicate challenges. Working unsustainable hours to meet unrealistic deadlines. Needs explicit permission to deliver bad news. Strengths: Dedication, precision. Create safe space for honest estimates.

She was starting to see a pattern. Victor needed recognition for his technical expertise and clear decision processes. Dmitri needed permission to be honest about limitations and timelines. Both were valuable team members with important contributions, but their different communication styles and perspectives were creating friction instead of collaboration.

As Marcia reviewed her notes, an email notification appeared - Elizabeth Parker confirming their 2 pm call with a list of pointed questions about project status. Marcia winced, knowing she couldn't honestly provide the reassurances Elizabeth wanted. The project was in worse shape than she'd initially realised, with at least one key component substantially behind schedule.

She glanced toward Priya's desk, wondering about those specifications Dmitri had been waiting for. Each conversation revealed new connections and complications. The team wasn't just disconnected - they were actively avoiding difficult conversations, operating on different assumptions, and suffering in silence rather than acknowledging problems.

Before she could craft an adequate response to Elizabeth, Marcia needed to speak with the remaining team members. The full picture was still emerging, and she suspected there were more silent struggles beneath the surface that needed to be brought into the light.

✧   ✧   ✧

Marcia spotted Mei returning to her desk, balancing a tray with several coffee cups. As she watched, Mei delivered them one by one - placing a cup on Victor's desk with a cheerful "Just how you like it, two sugars," dropping another by Dmitri with a gentle "Thought you could use this," and distributing the rest to Jason and Priya with personalised comments for each.

This small gesture of thoughtfulness confirmed what Marcia had already sensed: Mei was the unofficial social glue of the team. After her illuminating conversations with Victor and Dmitri, Marcia was curious about Mei's perspective on the team dynamics.

She waited until Mei had settled at her desk before approaching.

"That was a nice thing you did with the coffee," Marcia said.

Mei looked up with a warm smile. "It's nothing. Just a little Monday pick-me-up. Everyone seems extra stressed today."

"Do you have a few minutes to chat? I'm trying to get a better understanding of how everyone works together."

"Of course!" Mei's enthusiasm was immediate. "Let me just finish this email..."

Minutes later, they were walking through the office building's small atrium, a plant-filled space that few people used despite its pleasant atmosphere. Sunlight filtered through the skylights, a rare break in Seattle's ever-present mist.

"I love it here," Mei said, settling onto a bench surrounded by potted ferns. As they sat down, Mei automatically adjusted the placement of her coffee cup and notebook - a small ritual that centred her thoughts. There was something different in her posture today, a subtle straightening of her spine that suggested she was preparing to say something she'd been thinking about for a while. "It's so peaceful. I sometimes come down when I need to think through a problem."

"It is nice," Marcia agreed, taking in the green space. "How long have you been with the team, Mei?"

"Almost two years now. I've seen people come and go, but the current group has been together about eight months, except for Thomas who just joined us."

"And how would you describe how the team works together?"

Mei's bright expression dimmed slightly. "We used to collaborate really well. Everyone has different strengths, you know? Victor knows the system architecture inside and out. Dmitri can make databases sing. Jason has this incredible eye for UI details."

"But something changed?" Marcia prompted.

Mei sighed. "The FreshWorks project has been challenging. Carl tried his best, but there was so much pressure from the client. He started making promises we couldn't keep, and then..." She trailed off, looking uncomfortable.

"Then what?"

"Then he'd tell each of us different things to get us to agree," Mei admitted reluctantly. "He'd tell Victor one timeline for planning, then tell Dmitri another for client updates. Eventually, everyone realised what was happening, and trust just... evaporated."

"That explains a lot," Marcia said, thinking about the contradictory information she'd been gathering.

"I've tried to keep everyone connected," Mei continued. "Little things like coffee runs or bringing snacks. I started a team lunch tradition on Fridays - though lately, most people eat at their desks."

"Why do you make that effort?" Marcia asked, genuinely curious.

Mei looked surprised by the question. "Because we're better together than apart. I've seen what this team can do when everyone's aligned. It's amazing! The FreshWorks concept phase was like that - everyone contributing their best ideas, building on each other's work."

"What do you think changed?"

"Pressure," Mei said without hesitation. "When expectations got unrealistic, everyone retreated to their corners. Victor focused on technical correctness, Dmitri on meeting deadlines at any cost, others on just keeping their heads down."

The insight was astute. "And what about you?" Marcia asked. "How do you approach your work?"

Mei hesitated. "I try to be the bridge, I guess. When Victor and Dmitri clash, I try to find the middle ground. When the client is unhappy, I look for solutions that might work for everyone."

"That's a valuable skill," Marcia noted.

"Maybe," Mei said with uncharacteristic uncertainty. "But sometimes I wonder if I should push harder for my own technical ideas instead of always looking for compromise."

"What makes you hesitate?"

Mei's gaze dropped to her hands. "Confidence, I guess. The others are so certain about their approaches. I see multiple ways things could work, but I second-guess myself. Is my solution really the best one? Could I defend it as well as Victor defends his?"

Marcia recognised this pattern - a highly competent professional whose thoughtfulness was sometimes mistaken for indecision. "From what I've seen of your code, you should have plenty of confidence in your technical abilities."

"Thank you," Mei said, brightening slightly. "That means a lot coming from you. Your integration system last year was brilliant."

"That's the second time today someone's mentioned that project," Marcia said with a small laugh. "I'm starting to think I should put it on my resume."

"You absolutely should! We all admired how you handled that project - clear communication, solid technical decisions, on time despite all the obstacles."

This was surprising information. "I didn't realise people were paying attention to my work."

"Of course we were! That's why - " Mei stopped suddenly.

"Why what?"

"Well... why several of us were actually relieved when we heard you'd be taking over from Carl," Mei admitted. "We've seen how you work."

Marcia felt an unexpected warmth at this vote of confidence. "I appreciate that, though I'm still finding my footing in this role."

"You're doing great so far," Mei assured her. "You're actually listening to people. That's rarer than you think."

They sat in comfortable silence for a moment before Marcia returned to her information-gathering. "Can I ask about Priya? Dmitri mentioned he's waiting on specifications from her."

Mei's expression grew concerned. "Priya's overwhelmed. She's trying to finalise requirements for three different modules simultaneously, and Elizabeth keeps changing the priorities. I've tried to help where I can, but..."

"But it's not your assigned responsibility," Marcia finished.

"Exactly. And in this environment, everyone's protective of their domain." Mei hesitated, then added, "There's something you should know about the team structure. On paper, we're all equal developers with different focus areas. But in practice, Carl created an unofficial hierarchy."

"What do you mean?"

"Victor was treated as the technical lead, even though that wasn't his title. His opinions carried more weight on architecture decisions. Dmitri was the go-to for database work. I was..." Mei paused, searching for the right words, "I was the one Carl would send to smooth things over when other teams were upset with us."

"Because you're good with people," Marcia suggested.

"Because I'm a woman," Mei corrected gently. "Don't get me wrong - I enjoy cross-team collaboration. But sometimes I felt pigeonholed into the 'people person' role when I wanted more technical challenges."

Marcia made a note about this. The unofficial power structure explained some of the tensions she'd observed. "Thank you for your candour. Is there anything else I should know before my call with Elizabeth?"

Mei thought for a moment. "Yes - Elizabeth responds best to honesty, even when the news isn't good. Carl's approach of telling her what she wanted to hear just made things worse when deadlines were missed. She'd rather have a clear picture, even if it's not ideal."

"That's helpful," Marcia said, making another note. "One last question - what would help you be most effective in your role right now?"

Unlike Victor and Dmitri, who had needed time to consider this question, Mei answered immediately: "Clarity about where we're heading as a team, and more opportunities to contribute technically, not just as a peacemaker."

As they walked back to the main office area, Marcia reflected on how different each team member's needs were. Victor needed structure and recognition of his expertise. Dmitri needed realistic timelines and permission to be honest about challenges. Mei needed clearer direction and opportunities to showcase her technical skills beyond her peace-making abilities.

Seated once more at her desk, Marcia added to her notes:

Mei: Natural bridge-builder and empathetic colleague. Technical skills potentially underutilised. Needs: Recognition for technical contributions, not just interpersonal skills. Strengths: Seeing multiple perspectives, building consensus.

She was beginning to understand why the team was struggling. It wasn't just the absence of leadership - it was the lack of a system that acknowledged and utilised everyone's strengths while addressing their individual needs. Carl's management style had created an environment where people retreated to isolated work rather than true collaboration.

Marcia glanced at the clock - 1:30 pm. She didn't have time to speak with Jason, Priya, or Thomas before her call with Elizabeth. She'd have to go into that conversation with incomplete information, which wasn't ideal. But thanks to her conversations with Victor, Dmitri, and Mei, she at least had a clearer picture of the underlying issues.

The project wasn't just behind schedule - it was built on a foundation of misaligned expectations, unclear priorities, and unofficial hierarchies. Fixing those systemic problems would take more than a simple schedule adjustment or resource reallocation.

As she prepared for her call with Elizabeth, Marcia returned to the Team Leaders Toolbox documents James had provided. The section on team goals suddenly seemed more relevant than ever. Before she could realign the team on how to work together, they needed a shared understanding of what they were working toward.

Her computer pinged with a calendar reminder: fifteen minutes until the client call. Marcia took a deep breath, reviewing her notes one more time. Elizabeth Parker was expecting reassurances about timelines that Marcia couldn't honestly provide. But perhaps what Elizabeth really needed wasn't false promises, but a transparent assessment and a clear plan forward.

It was time to put Mei's insight to the test. Honesty over false comfort, reality over wishful thinking. Marcia just hoped Elizabeth would appreciate that approach as much as Mei believed she would.

✧　✧　✧

Marcia's office phone rang precisely at 2:00 pm. She took a deep breath and answered, "Elizabeth, hello. Thanks for making time today."

"Marcia." Elizabeth's crisp voice came through the speaker. "I understand congratulations are in order on your promotion to team lead."

"Thank you, though it's been a crash course so far," Marcia replied, trying to strike a balance between confidence and honesty.

"I'm sure." There was a rustling of papers on the other end. "Let's get right to it. I've been receiving conflicting information about the project status for weeks. Now that Carl's gone, I need a straight answer - are we on track for delivery next month?"

Marcia had anticipated this direct question. During the past hour, she'd reviewed Dmitri's task breakdown, which had arrived in her inbox with remarkable speed after their conversation. The picture it painted was concerning. Even without the authentication system changes, they were behind schedule on critical components.

Marcia glanced at her notebook again. She'd rewritten the talking points three times, and now abandoned them completely. What if she froze mid-sentence? What if Elizabeth saw right through her? She inhaled sharply, grounding herself in the one thing she could control: honesty.

"Elizabeth, I've spent my first day doing a comprehensive review, and I need to be candid with you," Marcia began. "Based on the current state of the project, we won't meet the original timeline with the full scope as defined."

The silence that followed felt interminable.

"I see," Elizabeth finally said, her tone cooling noticeably. "And when exactly were you planning to inform me of this?"

"Today, on this call," Marcia replied evenly. "I wanted to have accurate information before discussing it with you."

"Accurate information." Elizabeth repeated the words slowly. "Something Carl seemed incapable of providing. Do you have any idea how this affects our business planning? We have store managers waiting for this system."

"I understand the impact, which is why I'm not going to make promises I can't keep," Marcia said. "What I can offer instead is a realistic assessment and some options for moving forward."

Another silence, then: "I'm listening."

Marcia pulled out the notes she'd prepared. "We have three options as I see it. First, we can maintain the original delivery date but reduce scope to core functionality only, deferring some features to a phase two release. Second, we can keep the full scope but extend the timeline by three weeks. Or third, we can add resources to the team to try to meet somewhere in the middle."

"Those all sound like compromises, Marcia. My executives were promised a complete solution by the original date."

"They were," Marcia acknowledged. "And that was a promise that shouldn't have been made given the project complexity and available resources."

"So I'm supposed to go back to them and explain that Alpha Consulting can't deliver what was contracted?" Elizabeth's frustration was evident.

Marcia considered her next words carefully. "You're supposed to go back to them with accurate information so that FreshWorks can make an informed business decision. Would you rather I continued Carl's approach of telling you what you want to hear, only to disappoint you at the delivery date?"

The question hung in the air. Then, unexpectedly, Elizabeth laughed - a short, surprised sound.

"Well, that's refreshingly blunt," she said, her tone shifting slightly. "No, I wouldn't prefer that. What I would prefer is for someone to have had this conversation with me six weeks ago."

"I wish that had happened too," Marcia said. "But we're here now, and I'm committed to finding the best path forward."

"Tell me more about these options," Elizabeth said, her voice now more measured. "What exactly would be deferred in the reduced scope scenario?"

For the next twenty minutes, they discussed specifics. Marcia explained which features could reasonably be completed within the original timeframe, which would require more time, and what the dependencies were between different components. She was careful to frame everything in terms of business impact rather than technical challenges.

"The authentication system is a particular concern," Marcia explained. "The current approach works for your immediate needs, but would require significant rework when you expand internationally next year. We're recommending a more robust solution that will take additional time now but save months of redevelopment later."

"How do you know about our international expansion plans?" Elizabeth asked sharply.

"It was mentioned in the initial requirements gathering," Marcia replied, silently thanking Victor for his thorough explanation that morning. "It's one of the reasons we're concerned about some of the current architectural decisions."

Elizabeth was quiet for a moment. "Carl never raised these concerns."

"Different perspective, perhaps," Marcia offered diplomatically.

"Or different priorities," Elizabeth countered. "Look, Marcia, I appreciate your candour. It's actually a relief to have a clearer picture, even if it's not the one I wanted."

"So how would you like to proceed? Which option makes the most sense for FreshWorks?"

"None of them, ideally," Elizabeth said with a sigh. "But we live in reality, not ideality. Let me think about this and consult with our stakeholders. Can you send me a detailed breakdown of each option by tomorrow morning? I'll need specifics to present to our executive team."

"Absolutely," Marcia agreed, making a note. "I'll have that to you first thing."

"One more thing," Elizabeth added. "I'd like to institute weekly status updates - real ones, with actual progress metrics, not just reassurances. Would Wednesday mornings work for a standing call?"

"That works for me," Marcia said, relief washing over her. The conversation had gone better than expected. "I appreciate your understanding, Elizabeth."

"Don't mistake pragmatism for understanding," Elizabeth replied, though her tone had lost its earlier edge. "I'm still not happy about this situation. But I'd rather deal with uncomfortable truths than comfortable fictions. At least this way we can plan accordingly."

After they hung up, Marcia leaned back in her chair, exhaling slowly. The call had been tense, but ultimately productive. Elizabeth had responded to honesty exactly as Mei had predicted - with frustration, but also with a willingness to engage with reality rather than fantasy.

Her momentary relief was interrupted by the realisation of what she'd just committed to: a detailed analysis of three complex project options by tomorrow morning, plus a complete project reassessment for a weekly reporting cadence. She still hadn't spoken with Jason, Priya, or Thomas to understand their perspectives, and now she needed their input urgently.

A soft knock on her cubicle wall startled her. James stood there, eyebrows raised in question.

"How did it go?" he asked.

"Better than I feared, worse than I hoped," Marcia replied honestly. "Elizabeth isn't happy about the timeline issues, but she's willing to consider alternatives. I promised her a detailed analysis of options by tomorrow."

James nodded. "Good approach. Transparency from the start establishes the right foundation with clients, even when the news isn't ideal."

"That's what Mei suggested," Marcia said. "She seems to understand people remarkably well."

"She does," James agreed. "Have you spoken with everyone on the team yet?"

"Just Victor, Dmitri, and Mei so far. I still need to connect with Jason, Priya, and Thomas, but now I have this report to prepare for Elizabeth."

James considered this. "You could try a different approach. Instead of continuing one-on-ones, why not bring the team together to work on these options collaboratively? It would serve multiple purposes - gathering their input for Elizabeth's report while also giving you insight into how they interact and problem-solve together."

The suggestion made sense. "A working session rather than a formal meeting," Marcia mused. "That could work."

"It also sends a message about your leadership style," James pointed out. "Involving them in critical decisions rather than dictating solutions."

Marcia nodded, already thinking through the logistics. "I'll set it up for the end of day. That gives me time to prepare a framework for the discussion."

"Good. Let me know how it goes." James turned to leave, then added, "By the way, how did the technical meeting with Victor and Dmitri go this morning?"

"Surprisingly well," Marcia replied. "Once we established clear decision criteria, they actually found common ground. We're implementing Victor's authentication approach but with a phased rollout that addresses Dmitri's concerns about immediate deliverables."

James smiled. "You're finding your way faster than you think. Trust that process."

After he left, Marcia pulled out her notebook again, reviewing what she'd learned about the team so far. Each member had different perspectives, working styles, and needs - but they all wanted to deliver quality work. The dysfunction wasn't due to a lack of capability or commitment, but rather a lack of alignment and clear communication.

She drafted a meeting invitation for 4:30 pm, titled "FreshWorks Project Options - Working Session," and sent it to the entire team. Then she created a simple framework document outlining the three options they'd need to assess, with spaces for input on feasibility, risks, and resource needs.

As she worked, Marcia felt a subtle shift in her approach to the leadership role. On Friday, she'd been overwhelmed by the unexpected responsibility thrust upon her. Today, she was beginning to see how her analytical strengths could be applied to the human elements of the team, not just the technical challenges.

The team's diverse perspectives weren't obstacles to overcome - they were resources to leverage. Victor's technical rigor, Dmitri's focus on delivery, Mei's interpersonal awareness... each brought valuable insights that, properly aligned, could create something stronger than any individual contribution.

The upcoming working session would be her first real test in bringing these different perspectives together. It wasn't just about preparing a report for Elizabeth - it was about beginning to forge a cohesive team from a group of talented but disconnected individuals.

Marcia opened the Team Leaders Toolbox document again, focusing on the section about team goals. Before diving into the tactical options for the FreshWorks project, perhaps they needed to step back and align on some fundamental questions: What defined success for this project? What were they trying to achieve together?

With renewed purpose, she began preparing for the afternoon session, determined to build bridges across the differing perspectives that had kept this team fragmented for too long.

Chapter 3
Breaking Point

The afternoon working session had gone surprisingly well. The team had collaborated on Elizabeth's options report with more energy than Marcia had anticipated, each contributing valuable insights from their different perspectives. Even Victor and Dmitri had found common ground on several technical approaches. Marcia had left the office feeling cautiously optimistic about their path forward.

But that optimism evaporated the moment she walked into the office on Tuesday morning.

The first sign that something was wrong was the raised voices coming from the Enterprise Solutions area. As Marcia hurried toward the sound, she saw a small crowd gathered around Victor's workspace. Or rather, what had been Victor's workspace.

His desk had been moved about ten feet from its original position. The carefully arranged monitors were disconnected, reference books were stacked haphazardly, and the color-coded sticky note system lay scattered across the floor. In the centre of this chaos stood Victor, his face flushed with anger and distress.

" - absolutely unacceptable!" he was saying, his voice tight with barely controlled panic. "You had no right to move my workspace without consultation!"

A facilities manager Marcia didn't recognise stood opposite him, clipboard in hand, looking bewildered by the extreme reaction. "Sir, it's just a minor adjustment to accommodate the new network cabling - "

"Minor?" Victor's voice rose an octave. "You've destroyed my entire system! Every item was positioned precisely for optimal workflow. Do you have any idea how long it took to arrange everything?"

Mei hovered nearby, clearly trying to defuse the situation. "Victor, we can help you set everything back up exactly the way it was - "

"That's not the point!" Victor snapped, his hands clenching and unclenching at his sides. "The point is that no one bothered to inform me, let alone ask permission, before disrupting my work environment!"

The facilities manager looked to Marcia with relief as she approached. "Are you in charge here? We're just trying to complete the scheduled network upgrade."

Marcia took in the scene quickly. Victor was beyond merely upset - his breathing was rapid, his movements jerky, and he seemed overwhelmed by the situation. This wasn't just annoyance; it was genuine distress.

"I'm Marcia Hughes, the team leader," she said calmly. "Could you give us a few minutes, please? We'll sort this out."

The facilities manager nodded gratefully and retreated, muttering something about coming back later. The small crowd of onlookers began to disperse, sensing the show was over.

Marcia turned to Victor, careful to keep her voice low and even. "Victor, let's step away for a moment." She gestured toward the small conference room nearby.

He shook his head sharply. "I can't leave it like this. Everything is wrong."

"I understand," Marcia said, remembering his careful adjustments of the chairs yesterday. "What if Mei and I start putting things back while you take a short break?"

Victor seemed torn between the need to fix his workspace and the overwhelming nature of the task. His hands were trembling slightly.

"Mei knows where everything goes," Marcia added gently. "She pays attention to details."

This seemed to reach him. After a moment, Victor gave a curt nod and walked stiffly toward the break room.

Once he was out of earshot, Dmitri approached from his desk. "This is why I said we should tell him about the network upgrade yesterday," he said quietly. "But facilities said it wasn't confirmed yet."

"What exactly happened?" Marcia asked, already kneeling to gather the fallen sticky notes.

Mei joined her on the floor. "Facilities came in early this morning to run new network cables. They needed to move some desks to access the floor panels. Victor arrived to find everything already disarranged."

"For most people, it would be an annoyance," Dmitri added, his voice free of judgment. "For Victor, it is... more significant."

Marcia nodded, understanding better now. "Can you both help me restore his workspace? Mei, you said you know where things go?"

"More or less," Mei replied. She opened her mouth as if to add, "Next time we should push back on Facilities," but the words stalled when Victor's distress flashed back in her minds eye. Her voice softened instead. "Let's just get everything back the way he likes it."

"He keeps his monitors at precise angles, and his reference books are organised by a system only he fully understands, but I've watched him adjust things enough times to get close."

For the next fifteen minutes, they worked silently to recreate Victor's workspace as exactly as possible. Marcia was impressed by Mei's attention to detail - she knew precisely which monitor went where and even the specific angle of his keyboard.

As they finished reconnecting the equipment, Victor returned, looking marginally calmer but still visibly tense. He surveyed their work with a critical eye.

"The left monitor is three degrees too far right," he said, immediately adjusting it. "And these books are not in the correct order." He quickly rearranged several volumes.

"We did our best," Marcia said, watching as he made minute adjustments to each item on his desk. "I'm sorry this happened without warning."

Victor's hands paused briefly. "You did not authorise this?"

"No, I didn't know about it either. But that's not an excuse - as team leader, I should have been informed and made sure you were notified in advance."

This acknowledgment seemed to ease some of his tension. Victor continued methodically arranging his workspace, his movements becoming more fluid as order was restored.

"The facilities team needs to complete the network upgrade," Marcia explained carefully. "But I'll make sure they work with you on timing and approach, so nothing gets moved without your knowledge again."

Victor nodded, still focused on his adjustments. "That would be... helpful."

Mei and Dmitri drifted back to their desks, leaving Marcia alone with Victor. She waited patiently as he completed his arrangements, sensing that rushing him would only increase his stress.

Finally, Victor sat down in his chair, surveying his restored workspace with a critical eye. Most of the redness had faded from his face, but his posture remained rigid.

"Is there anything else you need?" Marcia asked.

Victor hesitated, then said quietly, "No. Thank you for your assistance."

"Victor," Marcia said carefully, "I'd like to understand better how to prevent situations like this in the future. Would it help if changes to your workspace were communicated in writing beforehand, with specific details about what will happen and when?"

He looked up, surprise flitting across his features. "Yes. That would be... very helpful. Especially if the notice included the exact nature of the changes and the expected duration."

"I'll make sure that happens," Marcia promised. "And I apologise again for the disruption."

Victor turned back to his computer, but before Marcia could walk away, he added, "Most people think I'm overreacting to trivial matters."

"It's not trivial if it affects your ability to work effectively," Marcia replied. "Different people have different needs. Part of my job is to understand those needs."

Something in Victor's expression softened almost imperceptibly. He gave a small nod and turned to his computer, clearly ready to reclaim his focus on work.

As Marcia walked back to her desk, she saw James standing nearby, having apparently witnessed the latter part of the interaction. He gave her an approving nod before continuing on his way.

At her desk, Marcia opened her notebook and added more observations about Victor:

Environment sensitivity - needs stability and predictability in physical workspace. Advance notice of changes critical. Becomes visibly distressed when routines disrupted. Recovers well when order is restored and concerns acknowledged.

She glanced toward Victor, now deeply focused on his work again, all traces of the earlier distress gone. The incident had been disruptive, but it had also revealed important information about how to work effectively with one of her key team members.

Her phone lit up with a text from James: *Good handling of the situation. See me when you have a moment.*

Before she could respond, her email pinged with a notification. Elizabeth Parker had replied to the options report Marcia had sent first thing that morning:

Marcia,

Discussed with executive team. Option 2 (full scope with extended timeline) is preferred. Need detailed revised schedule by EOD Thursday. Weekly status meetings confirmed for 10 am Wednesdays.

Regards,

Elizabeth

Marcia leaned back in her chair, processing the implications. The good news: they had a decision and could move forward. The challenging news: she now needed to create a detailed project schedule in just two days, which meant understanding the full scope of work across all team members.

Victor's meltdown had been unexpected but manageable. What worried her more were the issues she hadn't yet uncovered with the team members she hadn't had time to speak with individually. Jason and Priya had contributed to yesterday's working session, but neither had volunteered much about their specific challenges. And Thomas, the QA analyst, had remained almost entirely silent.

Marcia flicked through the pages of the Team Leaders Toolbox to the section on conducting a skills matrix assessment. Understanding each team member's capabilities, current workload, and constraints would be essential for creating a realistic schedule - and this looked like the right tool for the capability assessment.

The Victor situation had made one thing abundantly clear: she couldn't apply a one-size-fits-all approach to this team. Each member had unique needs and working styles that needed to be acknowledged and accommodated for the team to function effectively.

As if reading her thoughts, her calendar pinged with a new appointment from James for later that afternoon: "Leadership Discussion: Team Assessment." It seemed her mentor was one step ahead, anticipating her next challenge.

Marcia began drafting a team-wide email about the project direction, already thinking about how to structure the revised schedule development process. The morning's drama had been a setback, but also an opportunity - a vivid demonstration of why understanding individual team dynamics wasn't just a nice-to-have, but essential for their collective success.

✧ ✧ ✧

The morning's chaos with Victor had barely settled when Thomas Nguyen appeared at Marcia's desk, tablet in hand and a concerned expression on his face.

"Do you have a minute?" he asked quietly. "There's something you should see."

As the newest addition to the team, Thomas had remained almost silent during yesterday's working session. Marcia was eager to understand his perspective.

"Of course," she replied, gesturing to the chair beside her desk.

Thomas sat and opened his tablet. "I've completed initial testing on the database components Dmitri delivered yesterday. The results are... concerning."

Thomas exhaled through his nose, a sharp breath he hadn't meant to be audible, then folded his arms tightly - almost bracing himself for the reaction.

He slid her the tablet, displaying a detailed test report. Red error indicators dominated the screen.

"Twenty-eight critical defects?" Marcia scanned the document with growing alarm. "This can't be right. Dmitri's work is usually precise."

"That was my understanding as well," Thomas agreed. "Which is why I ran the tests twice and then manually verified the most serious issues."

Marcia scrolled through the report, her concern deepening. Missing data validations, incorrect field mappings, incomplete transaction handling - these weren't minor oversights but fundamental problems.

"Have you shared this with Dmitri yet?"

Thomas shifted uncomfortably. "No. Under Carl's leadership, the protocol was to report quality issues to the team lead first. Carl would then... filter what was communicated to the developers."

Marcia frowned. "Filter how, exactly?"

"He would categorise defects as 'must-fix' or 'nice-to-have,'" Thomas explained. "Often downgrading critical issues if addressing them would impact the timeline."

"That ends now," Marcia said firmly. "Quality isn't optional. Let's talk to Dmitri together."

They found Dmitri hunched at his desk, dark circles under his eyes despite Marcia's directive to rest over the weekend. When he saw them approaching with the tablet, his expression became guarded.

"Dmitri, Thomas has completed testing on yesterday's database delivery," Marcia began carefully. "There are some quality concerns we need to discuss."

As Thomas walked through the findings, Dmitri's stoic facade crumbled. He slumped in his chair, eyes fixed on his keyboard.

"May I see the report?" he finally asked, voice barely audible.

Thomas handed him the tablet. Dmitri scanned it, his expression unreadable.

"These are legitimate issues," he acknowledged after a long pause. "I will fix them."

"That's not the only concern," Marcia said gently. "This level of defects is unexpected from you. What's happening?"

Dmitri remained silent for so long that Marcia wondered if he'd answer. Finally, he spoke, his accent thickening with emotion.

"I have been working sixteen-hour days for weeks. The specifications keep changing. I am trying to meet impossible deadlines." He gestured at the defect report. "This is the result."

Marcia glanced at the timestamp on the code delivery: 11:47 pm.

"You were here until midnight?" she asked.

Dmitri shrugged slightly. "Later. I had to finish."

Thomas looked uncomfortable. "I didn't realise - "

"How could you?" Dmitri interrupted without hostility. "No one sees. No one is supposed to see. Just deliver on time, that is all that matters."

Marcia thought back to their conversation yesterday. She'd told him to take the weekend off, but clearly the damage from weeks of overwork was already done.

"I need to understand the full picture," she said. "Thomas, can you give us a moment?"

After Thomas departed, Marcia pulled up a chair. "Dmitri, talk to me honestly. How long have you been working at this pace?"

"Since the project began," he admitted. "Carl said the timeline was non-negotiable. When I could not keep up, he suggested I 'find extra hours.'"

"So, you've been working every night and weekend for six weeks straight, not just some?"

Dmitri nodded. "At first, just a few extra hours. Then more. The specifications kept changing, but the deadlines did not."

"And the quality issues?"

"I review code at 2 am. I miss things." His voice carried both shame and defiance. "What choice did I have? The client expects miracles."

Marcia thought about the defect report. These weren't simple mistakes from fatigue - they reflected a systematic breakdown from sustained overwork.

"This isn't sustainable," she said. "Not for you, and not for the project. Quality matters."

"You think I don't know this?" For the first time, frustration edged into Dmitri's voice. "I take pride in my work. But when forced to choose between 'on time with defects' or 'late but perfect,' the message has always been clear."

Marcia realised she was facing not just a quality issue but a cultural one. Under Carl's leadership, the team had been conditioned to prioritise deadlines over everything - including their own wellbeing and the integrity of their work.

"We're changing that message," she said firmly. "I spoke with Elizabeth yesterday. We're extending the timeline to deliver the full scope correctly."

Dmitri looked up after a time, wary hope in his tired eyes. His shoulders rose, then set. "She agreed to this?"

"Yes. And now I need your help creating a realistic schedule - one that allows for quality work within standard hours."

She paused, then added deliberately, "I'd rather have honest estimates that we can meet with quality than impossible deadlines that drive us to cut corners."

Dmitri studied her face, as if searching for insincerity. "Carl said the same at first."

"I'm not Carl," Marcia replied simply. "And I'll prove that through actions, not just words."

She stood. "First action: go home. Now. Get some real rest and take tomorrow off if you need to. The defects can wait."

"But - "

"That's not a suggestion, Dmitri. It's a direction." Her tone was kind but firm. "A team working sustainable hours produces better results than individuals burning themselves out."

After Dmitri reluctantly gathered his things and left, Marcia returned to her desk, troubled by what she'd discovered. She pulled out her notebook and added:

Quality issues surfacing - direct result of unsustainable pace. Team culture values deadlines over wellbeing and quality. Need to establish new norms and expectations. Unrealistic timelines → cutting corners → defects → more work later.

She glanced at the Team Leaders Toolbox folder. The section on skills matrix suddenly seemed insufficient. She needed a deeper understanding of the team's capacity, workload distribution, and how tasks were actually being performed - not just who could theoretically do what.

Picking up her phone, she texted James: *Need to talk about resource allocation and quality standards. Team has been working unsustainably.*

His reply came quickly: *Suspected as much. Our 3pm still on. Bring what you've found.*

As Marcia prepared for her meeting with James, she noticed Thomas and Priya in an intense conversation across the office. Their gestures suggested disagreement, and when Sarah Williams from the business analysis team joined them, the discussion grew more animated.

The quality issues with Dmitri's work were just the visible symptoms of deeper problems. If his components were this compromised, what other issues might be lurking beneath the surface of the FreshWorks project?

✧　✧　✧

Marcia had just finished reviewing Dmitri's defect report when she noticed Sarah Williams striding purposefully toward her desk. The business analyst's expression was a mix of determination and frustration that immediately put Marcia on alert.

"We need to talk," Sarah announced without preamble, crossing her arms. "Preferably somewhere private."

Marcia nodded, grabbing her notebook. "Conference Room B should be empty."

As they walked, Marcia studied Sarah from the corner of her eye. She'd had limited interactions with the analyst before, but knew her reputation as sharp, demanding, and relentlessly focused on business needs. The tension in Sarah's shoulders suggested this wouldn't be a casual conversation.

Once the door closed behind them, Sarah wasted no time. "I just spoke with Thomas and Priya about the timeline extension. Is it true you've already committed to pushing the delivery date without consulting the business team?"

Marcia took a measured breath. "I presented Elizabeth with several options based on our current status. She chose the extended timeline."

"That's not how this works," Sarah countered, her voice rising slightly. "Business requirements drive technical decisions, not the other way around. You can't just arbitrarily move deadlines because your team finds the work challenging."

"There's nothing arbitrary about this decision," Marcia replied evenly. "The timeline was extended because the original one was unrealistic given the scope and available resources."

Sarah's eyebrows shot up. "Unrealistic? We've been working toward this deadline for months!" Her voice carried an edge that seemed disproportionate to the situation. "My manager specifically asked me to ensure this project stays on track. That timeline's ambitious... but I'll make it work. I always do." The words came out defensive, almost rehearsed, as if she'd given this speech before. "My FreshWorks stakeholders have already scheduled training, marketing communications, even a launch event."

"I understand your frustration - "

"No, I don't think you do," Sarah interrupted. "Do you know what happens when we miss our market window? Competitors gain ground. Revenue projections fall short. And guess who takes the blame? Not the development team that couldn't deliver. It's the business team that 'failed to plan properly.'"

The words landed like a gavel, and Sarah felt a knot tighten behind her ribs. Great, she thought, *one more miss and the BA leadership will pin this whole thing on me.* A cool mask slid back over her face before anyone could notice.

Marcia waited a moment to ensure Sarah had finished. "I appreciate the business pressures you're under. But there's something you should know about the current state of the project."

She opened her notebook and laid out the facts: Dmitri's quality issues stemming from unsustainable overtime, the authentication system that would require complete reworking if rushed, and the incomplete specifications that were causing rework across multiple components.

"These aren't excuses," Marcia emphasised. "They're realities. The choice isn't between delivering on time or extending the deadline. It's between extending now with a clear plan, or pretending we're on track until everything falls apart at the last minute."

Sarah's expression shifted slightly. "Why am I only hearing about these issues now?"

"That's a fair question," Marcia acknowledged. "From what I've gathered, there's been a culture of telling people what they want to hear rather than confronting difficult truths."

Sarah uncrossed her arms and sank into a chair. "Carl assured me last week that everything was on track except for 'minor technical adjustments.'"

"Those 'minor adjustments' include twenty-eight critical defects in just one component," Marcia said gently. "And that's what we've found after only two days of proper testing."

Sarah rubbed her temples. "This is a disaster. Elizabeth may have agreed to the extension, but my stakeholders won't be nearly as understanding."

She paused, ready to deliver another cutting remark, but something in Marcia's steady gaze gave her pause. "Unless..." The word hung in the air as Sarah's expression shifted almost imperceptibly. "Unless you've got a better idea, Marcia?" The question carried the faintest hint of respect, as if she was testing whether this new team leader might actually be different.

"What if we worked together on this?" Marcia suggested. "Instead of development making unilateral technical decisions and business making unilateral requirement decisions, what if we approached this as a shared challenge?"

Sarah looked sceptical. "What exactly are you proposing?"

"A joint reassessment," Marcia explained. "We look at the business priorities alongside the technical realities and create a plan that delivers the most critical functionality first, with the highest quality."

"A phased approach," Sarah mused. "It's not ideal, but..." She paused, considering. "I could position the extension as giving us the opportunity to incorporate additional market feedback before the full rollout."

"Exactly," Marcia nodded. "And we could potentially deliver a limited beta to key stakeholders on the original timeline, giving them something tangible while we complete the full solution."

For the first time, Sarah's expression lightened slightly, the defensive armour she'd worn in earlier in the conversation seeming to crack just a little. "Look, I've been burned before by teams that overpromise," she said, her tone softer than usual. "but you actually seem to care. That's refreshing." There was something almost vulnerable in the admission, as if she was allowing herself to hope. "That might actually work. The VP of Operations has been asking for early access anyway."

They spent the next twenty minutes outlining a potential approach, with Sarah identifying the highest-priority business functions while Marcia noted which components were most stable.

"I'll need to bring this back to my team," Sarah said, gathering her notes. "But this is a much better conversation than I expected to have."

As they prepared to leave, Sarah paused at the door. "You know, Carl never once invited me to collaboratively solve a problem. It was always either 'yes, we can do that' or 'that's technically impossible' with nothing in between."

"Different approach," Marcia said with a small smile.

"A better one," Sarah admitted. "But don't think this means I won't push hard for what my stakeholders need. That's still my job."

"I'd be disappointed if you didn't," Marcia replied. "Just as it's my job to push for what the development team needs to deliver quality work."

Returning to her desk, Marcia added to her growing notes:

Sarah: Direct, business-focused, under pressure from stakeholders. Needs: Clear communication, involvement in technical decisions with business impact, help managing stakeholder expectations. Opportunity: Could be powerful ally if brought into solution development rather than just requirement setting.

The confrontation with Sarah had triggered an uncomfortable memory - a leadership meeting two years ago where she'd sat silent while two senior leaders argued about a technical decision she knew was wrong. She'd had the expertise to speak up, the data to back her position, but the words had stuck in her throat. Later, watching that technical approach fail exactly as she'd predicted, she'd sworn she'd never stay quiet again when she knew better.

But knowing better about technical issues was different from knowing better about people. With Sarah, she'd felt that same familiar paralysis creeping in - the voice that whispered she didn't belong in these conversations, that she should stick to what she knew. The difference was, this time she'd pushed through it. Not gracefully, maybe, but she'd pushed through.

She had just finished writing when her phone chimed with a text from James: *Ready for our 3pm?*

Marcia gathered her notes, increasingly aware of the complexity of the challenge she faced. The technical issues were serious, but they were symptoms of deeper problems: misaligned expectations, poor communication channels, unsustainable work practices, and a culture of avoiding difficult conversations.

As she headed toward James's office, she noticed Victor and Mei engaged in what appeared to be a detailed discussion about system architecture. They were actually speaking civilly, with Victor pointing to a diagram while Mei asked thoughtful questions. It was a small sign of potential team cohesion - a bright spot in an otherwise challenging day.

The conversation with Sarah had been unexpectedly productive, despite its tense beginning. Perhaps the path forward wasn't about resolving individual conflicts or fixing isolated technical problems, but about creating a fundamentally different way for the team to work together - one built on transparency, realistic expectations, and genuine collaboration.

✧ ✧ ✧

James looked up from his desk and gestured Marcia in with a smile. She took a deep breath, ready to share what she'd discovered and hoping her mentor would have insights on how to address not just the symptoms, but the underlying causes of the team's problems.

"Rough day?" James asked as Marcia sank into the chair across from his desk.

"You could say that." She pushed her hair back with a sigh. "In the past eight hours, I've dealt with Victor having a meltdown over his desk being moved, discovered Dmitri's been working sixteen-hour days and producing defect-ridden code as a result, and had a confrontation with Sarah from the business team about the timeline extension."

James leaned back in his chair. "So, Tuesday is going well, then?"

Despite everything, Marcia laughed. "Spectacularly."

"Tell me more about what you've discovered," James prompted, pushing aside the papers on his desk to give her his full attention.

Over the next fifteen minutes, Marcia detailed everything she'd learned about the team's dynamics and challenges. James listened intently, occasionally asking clarifying questions but mostly letting her talk.

"The technical issues I can handle," Marcia concluded. "But it's the people issues that have me worried. Victor needs structure and predictability. Dmitri is exhausted and afraid to push back on unrealistic deadlines. Mei is being pigeonholed as the 'people person' when she wants technical challenges. And that's just the team members I've had time to really talk with."

She pulled out her notebook, showing James her growing collection of observations. "I feel like I'm uncovering new problems faster than I can solve the existing ones."

"Welcome to leadership," James said with a wry smile. "The problems never stop coming. The trick is learning which ones need your immediate attention and which ones can wait."

"That's the thing," Marcia said, frustration edging into her voice. "They all seem urgent. The quality issues are jeopardising delivery. The unrealistic deadlines are burning people out. The communication gaps are causing constant misunderstandings." She closed her notebook. "I'm starting to think Carl didn't leave for a startup opportunity - he fled a sinking ship."

James considered her for a moment. "Do you know why I recommended you for this role?"

Marcia shook her head. "I've been wondering that myself, especially today."

"Because when you approach a complex technical problem, you don't just dive in with a quick fix. You step back, analyse the system as a whole, identify root causes, and develop a structured approach." James leaned forward. "That's exactly what this team needs - someone who can see beyond the immediate fires to address the underlying systemic issues."

"But technical problems have logical solutions," Marcia countered. "People are... messier."

"Are they, though?" James pulled a wheeled whiteboard toward them. "Let's try something. If this were a technical system showing these symptoms, how would you approach it?"

Marcia thought for a moment, then picked up a marker. "I'd start by mapping the components and their interfaces." She began drawing boxes labelled with team members' names and lines showing their interactions. "Then I'd identify failure points in the system."

She added notes about the issues she'd discovered: Victor's need for predictable processes, Dmitri's unsustainable workload, the quality issues, the communication gaps with business stakeholders.

"Good," James nodded. "And once you've mapped the system and identified failure points, what next?"

"Prioritise the most critical failures," Marcia said, circling Dmitri's situation and the quality issues. "Then develop interventions that address root causes, not just symptoms."

As she continued diagramming, Marcia felt her perspective shifting. The team's dysfunction wasn't a chaotic mess of personality conflicts and individual problems - it was a system with clear patterns, feedback loops, and failure modes. Viewed this way, the path forward became clearer.

"I think I see what you're getting at," she said, stepping back from the whiteboard. "The same analytical approach I use for technical systems can work here, just with different variables."

"Exactly," James confirmed. "You don't need to become a different person to lead effectively. Use the strengths you already have."

Marcia studied the diagram she'd created. "The biggest systemic issue is the disconnect between expectations and reality. Carl created unrealistic expectations with Elizabeth, which forced impossible deadlines on the team, which led to burnout and quality issues, which will ultimately delay delivery even more."

"So where would you intervene in that cycle?" James asked.

"At multiple points," Marcia replied, drawing stars on the whiteboard. "Set realistic expectations with Elizabeth - already started that. Create sustainable workloads for the team. Establish quality standards and processes. Improve communication channels between technical and business teams."

She looked at James. "But I can't do all of this at once. The immediate crisis is Dmitri's burnout and the quality issues."

"Good prioritisation," James nodded. "Address the critical failures first, then work on longer-term system improvements."

Marcia felt a weight lifting from her shoulders. The challenges were still daunting, but now they seemed manageable - problems to be solved methodically rather than an overwhelming flood.

"There's one other thing," James added. "You don't have to solve all these problems alone. In fact, you shouldn't. Part of being a leader is empowering your team to solve problems together."

"Like the working session yesterday," Marcia realised. "They actually collaborated quite well when given a clear framework."

"People want to do good work," James said. "Most team dysfunction comes from systems that prevent that, not from the people themselves."

Marcia glanced at her watch and stood. "I should check on Victor before the end of day. He seemed okay after we restored his workspace, but I want to make sure."

"Good instinct," James agreed. "Quick check-ins show you're paying attention without micromanaging."

At the door, Marcia turned back. "Thank you. For recommending me for this role and for helping me see it differently."

"You're doing better than you think," James replied. He paused, thumb tapping the desk once before he spoke again. "Truth is, when you talk through a problem like that, I hear the lieutenant I used to be - keen, analytical, still learning which battles matter most."

He looked her in the eye, "When the field turns to smoke and chaos," James said, letting the words settle, "an experienced captain climbs the nearest ridge, surveys every flank, and moves only the units that shift the battle. That's leadership - choosing the few decisive batteries, not firing every cannon at once."

Walking back to her team's area, Marcia felt renewed confidence. The challenges hadn't changed, but her perspective had. She wasn't just reacting to crises anymore; she was developing a systematic approach to transforming how the team functioned.

She spotted Victor at his desk, headphones on, fully absorbed in his work. His workspace was back to its precisely ordered state, and his posture was relaxed - a good sign. Nearby, Mei was helping Thomas set up a testing environment, their conversation punctuated by occasional laughter.

Small positive signs, but meaningful ones. The team had potential; they just needed the right structure and support to realise it.

Marcia headed to her desk to prepare for tomorrow. She needed to develop a more formal approach to understanding the team's skills, workloads, and processes. The Team Leaders Toolbox materials James had provided mentioned something about a skills matrix and team goals that seemed particularly relevant now.

As she worked, Marcia's phone buzzed with a calendar notification: *FreshWorks Project Review* with Robert Miller, Alpha Consulting's founder, scheduled for tomorrow morning. She hadn't even met Miller yet, and now she'd be presenting to him about a troubled project she'd only been leading for three days.

The moment of confidence wavered. But then she looked at the system diagram she'd created with James, took a deep breath, and reminded herself: analyse, prioritise, intervene strategically. One step at a time.

✦ ✦ ✦

Leaving that evening, Marcia noticed Mei had been working late too. Marcia sat in her car in the empty parking garage, engine off, hands clutching the steering wheel. The weight of the day - Victor's meltdown, Dmitri's exhaustion, the quality issues, Robert's meeting - crashed over her like a wave she'd been holding back all day.

Her phone buzzed. Another email from Elizabeth. Another request for reassurance she couldn't honestly give.

She pressed her forehead against the steering wheel and let out a sound somewhere between a laugh and a sob. Who was she kidding? She wasn't a leader. She was a developer playing dress-up in a role she'd never wanted.

Her phone buzzed again. This time a text from Mei: *Left a little potted jade on your desk. You're doing better than you realise. We really appreciate your effort.*

Marcia stared at the message, something shifting in her chest. Maybe she wasn't ready. Maybe she'd never feel ready. But Mei believed in her. James believed in her. Maybe that was enough for now.

She started the engine, Mei's simple kindness anchoring her back to what mattered. Tomorrow she'd try again.

Chapter 4
Vision Formation

Marcia arrived early Wednesday morning, determined to prepare for her meeting with Robert Miller. She had barely settled at her desk when James appeared, two coffee cups in hand.

"Thought you might need this," he said, placing one on her desk. "Heard you've got Miller at nine."

"News travels fast," Marcia replied, gratefully accepting the coffee. "Any advice for meeting the founder of the company when I'm about to tell him his most important client project is in trouble?"

James leaned against her desk. "Be straightforward. Robert appreciates honesty over sugar-coating. And come with at least the outline of a plan - he responds better to solutions than problems."

Marcia nodded, pulling up the system diagram she'd created yesterday. "I'm working on that part. The challenge is knowing where to start."

"That's actually why I stopped by," James said. "After our talk yesterday, I thought you might be ready for this." He placed a folder on her desk labelled "Team Goals Framework."

"Another tool from your leadership arsenal?" Marcia asked with a small smile.

"The most important one," James replied. "Before you can fix processes or assign responsibilities, you need alignment on what the team is trying to achieve together."

Marcia opened the folder to find a structured template with sections for mission statements, priority objectives, and success metrics. "This seems straightforward enough."

"The template is simple," James agreed. "The conversations it drives are anything but. When you ask people what success looks like, you uncover all sorts of misalignments and assumptions."

"Like Victor prioritising technical elegance while Dmitri focuses on meeting deadlines," Marcia observed.

"Exactly. Those aren't necessarily incompatible goals, but without a shared understanding of priorities, they become sources of conflict." James tapped the folder. "This framework helps make those implicit priorities explicit so the team can align on what matters most."

Marcia scanned the document. "So I should create these goals for the team?"

"Not for them - with them," James corrected. "The power of this approach isn't just the resulting document. It's the conversation that creates it. Everyone contributes, everyone's heard, and everyone commits to the outcome."

"I can see how that would help," Marcia said, thinking about the fragmented perspectives she'd encountered. "But we're in the middle of a crisis. Should I really be taking time for goal-setting exercises?"

"Especially then," James insisted. "Your team is pulling in different directions during the exact moment they need to be unified. Monday, you had a productive working session that briefly aligned everyone. Imagine what they could accomplish with permanent alignment."

Marcia wasn't entirely convinced. "Elizabeth is expecting a revised schedule tomorrow. Robert Miller wants a project update in an hour. We have critical quality issues to address. This feels like something that could wait until we're on more stable ground."

James smiled knowingly. "That's what every leader says. 'We'll define our vision after we handle this crisis.' But there's always another crisis. The teams that weather those storms are the ones with clear, shared direction."

He stood to leave. "Think about it. Your technical instincts are to define requirements before writing code. Team goals are your requirements specification for how the team operates."

After James left, Marcia flipped through the folder, reading the examples and instructions. The approach was more structured than she'd expected - not just vague aspirational statements but specific, prioritised objectives with clear success metrics.

She thought about her conversations with team members. Victor needed structure and recognition for his expertise. Dmitri needed sustainable workloads and permission to be honest about challenges. Mei wanted more technical opportunities while maintaining her connecting role. They all wanted to deliver quality work they could be proud of.

Maybe James was right. Maybe what they needed wasn't just better processes or clearer responsibilities, but a shared understanding of what they were trying to achieve together.

Her computer pinged with a calendar reminder: thirty minutes until her meeting with Robert Miller. She closed the folder, setting it aside for later. First, she needed to get through this meeting with a clear assessment of the project's status and the beginnings of a recovery plan.

As she considered possible approaches, Marcia noticed Victor arriving back from a break, nodding briefly to her before settling at his meticulously arranged workspace. Dmitri's desk remained empty - she'd insisted he take the day off after discovering his unsustainable schedule. Mei was already there, talking quietly with Thomas about the test environment.

They were good people, skilled professionals who wanted to succeed. The dysfunction wasn't coming from lack of capability or commitment, but from misalignment and unclear direction. James's team goals framework suddenly seemed less like a theoretical exercise and more like an essential foundation.

Marcia tucked the folder into her bag. She'd review it more carefully after her meeting with Miller. If that went well, perhaps she could introduce the concept to the team this afternoon.

As she headed toward the executive meeting room, Marcia felt her initial scepticism about the team goals approach fading. In its place was a growing recognition that before she could address the technical issues, resource constraints, or process problems, she needed to unite the team around a shared vision of success.

The elevator doors opened on the executive floor, revealing a very different environment from the practical workspaces below. Here, glass-walled offices and sleek conference rooms projected an image of confident professionalism that Marcia hoped she could match in her presentation.

Robert Miller's assistant looked up from her desk. "He's ready for you," she said, gesturing toward the corner office. "Good luck."

Taking a deep breath, Marcia mentally shifted gears from thinking about team goals to preparing for the immediate challenge ahead. But as she walked toward Miller's office, she realised the two weren't entirely separate. The clearer she could be about what success looked like for the FreshWorks project, the more effectively she could communicate both the problems and the path forward.

With renewed purpose, Marcia knocked on the door, ready to face the founder of Alpha Consulting and begin the process of transforming her fragmented group into a true team.

✦ ✦ ✦

Robert Miller was not what Marcia had expected. From the way people spoke about Alpha Consulting's founder, she'd imagined an intimidating executive with penetrating questions and little patience. Instead, she'd found a thoughtful listener with astute observations and a surprisingly deep understanding of technical challenges.

"Well, that went better than I anticipated," Marcia murmured to herself as she settled back into her desk chair.

The meeting had been straightforward. Miller had asked pointed questions about the FreshWorks project status, nodded thoughtfully at her honest assessment of the issues, and seemed genuinely appreciative of her early intervention.

"Better to reset expectations now than apologise for missed deadlines later," he'd said, echoing her own thoughts. His final words had stuck with her: "This team has tremendous potential. They just need the right direction."

Now, alone at her desk with a fresh cup of coffee, Marcia pulled out James's Team Goals Framework again. The concept made sense in theory, but how would it work in practice with a team already stretched thin by immediate challenges?

She opened her notebook to a blank page and began jotting down what she'd learned about each team member's implicit goals:

Victor: Technical excellence, proper architecture, recognition of expertise
Dmitri: Meeting commitments, efficiency, sustainable workload
Mei: Team harmony, technical growth, meaningful contribution

Thomas: Quality standards, proper testing processes
Priya: Clear requirements, manageable scope
Jason: [Still need to learn more]

The list revealed obvious tensions. Victor's pursuit of technical perfection often conflicted with Dmitri's focus on meeting deadlines. Mei's desire for team harmony sometimes meant her own technical ambitions took a back seat.

"No wonder they're pulling in different directions," Marcia muttered. "They're playing different games with different scorecards."

Her focus moved to the framework document, studying the structure James had outlined. It seemed to address exactly this issue - creating a shared definition of success that everyone could align around.

The conference room she'd booked for her afternoon meeting with the team was empty. A bulky conference phone sat in the centre of the table like a plastic starfish, used for the twice-weekly calls with the client when in-person meetings weren't possible. On one whiteboard, someone had scribbled notes from an earlier meeting along with a URL to a SharePoint folder containing project documents. Marcia arrived early, arranging chairs around the table and setting up a fresh whiteboard with the heading "Team Goals" across the top.

Should she start with a blank slate, letting the team build the goals from scratch? Or should she propose initial directions based on what she'd learned? The first approach might generate more ownership, but the second would be more efficient.

"Both," she decided, quickly sketching a basic framework on the whiteboard with spaces to fill in collaboratively.

As team members filtered in, Marcia noted their expressions - curiosity from Mei, wariness from Victor, fatigue from Dmitri despite being given the day off, he had a few hours extra sleep in the morning then returned to work, and neutral professionalism from Thomas and Jason. Priya arrived last, slightly breathless and clutching a stack of specification documents.

"Thanks for making time for this," Marcia began once everyone was seated. "I know you're all busy with immediate tasks, but after my conversations with each of you and this morning's executive review, I believe we need to take a step back and align on some fundamentals."

"Is this about the timeline extension?" Priya asked, a hint of worry in her voice.

"It's about much more than that," Marcia replied. "It's about how we work together as a team going forward."

Her glance moving between the whiteboard and the team. "Over the past few days, I've observed something interesting. We have tremendous talent in this room - deep expertise, commitment to quality, desire to deliver value to the client. But we don't have a shared understanding of what success looks like."

Victor shifted in his seat. "Success is delivering a properly architected solution that meets requirements."

"That's one aspect," Marcia acknowledged. "But there are others." She pointed to her notes. "Dmitri might define success as meeting commitments to clients. Mei might emphasise team collaboration and growth. Thomas focuses on quality standards."

"Those all sound important," Jason offered, speaking up at last. "Aren't they just different parts of the same goal?"

"They should be," Marcia agreed. "But without explicit agreement on priorities, they become competing interests rather than complementary aspects of a shared vision."

She passed out copies of a simplified goals template. "This isn't about creating bureaucratic paperwork. It's about having an honest conversation about what matters most to this team - both what we deliver and how we work together to deliver it."

Dmitri studied the document sceptically. "How will this help fix the immediate quality issues or timeline problems?"

"It won't - directly," Marcia conceded. "Those require specific technical and process interventions. But this will give us a foundation for making those decisions consistently, rather than constantly pulling in different directions."

To clarify further she added. "In our first meeting we mapped goals to tasks and timeline, and now I want us to think in terms of vision and priorities."

She uncapped a marker and approached the whiteboard. "Let me start with a question: When this project ends, what would make you feel proud of what we accomplished together?"

The room fell silent as team members considered the question. Then Mei spoke up, her voice soft but clear.

"I'd be proud if we delivered something that genuinely helps FreshWorks' employees do their jobs better."

Marcia wrote on the board: *Deliver genuine value to users*

"I would feel proud if we created a system with clean architecture that scales for future needs," Victor added.

Marcia added: *Build technically sound, scalable solutions*

One by one, each team member contributed. Thomas mentioned quality standards. Dmitri emphasised reliability. Priya brought up meeting user requirements. Jason talked about creating intuitive interfaces.

As the list grew, Marcia noticed something important - the tension in the room was easing. For perhaps the first time, team members weren't defending their individual territories but contributing to a collective vision.

"These are all excellent," Marcia said, stepping back from the now-filled whiteboard. "But we can't prioritise everything equally. If we had to focus on just three to five goals that represent our core priorities as a team, which would they be?"

This sparked a more animated discussion. Victor and Thomas advocated strongly for quality and technical excellence. Dmitri and Priya emphasised meeting commitments and user needs. Mei suggested balancing immediate delivery with sustainable pace.

Marcia facilitated without imposing her own views, asking clarifying questions and ensuring everyone was heard. Gradually, a consensus began to emerge around key priorities that balanced different perspectives.

As the meeting neared its scheduled end time, Marcia felt a shift in the room's energy. The initial scepticism had given way to engaged problem-solving. Even Victor and Dmitri, who had clashed most visibly before, were building on each other's points rather than contradicting them.

"This is a great start," Marcia said, taking a photo of the whiteboard. "I'll capture what we've discussed and circulate a draft for review. Then we can refine and finalise together."

As the team gathered their things to leave, Mei lingered behind.

"That was different," she said quietly. "Usually our meetings are just status updates or technical debates. This felt more foundational."

"That's exactly what it is," Marcia replied. "We're building the foundation for how we work together."

After everyone had left, Marcia remained in the conference room, studying the whiteboard covered with the team's thoughts and priorities. The exercise had revealed both common ground and areas that needed more alignment.

The beginnings of a true team identity were emerging from what had been a collection of skilled individuals working in proximity rather than in concert. There was still a long way to go, but at last, since accepting the leadership role, Marcia felt they were moving in the right direction - together.

As she transferred the whiteboard notes to her laptop, Marcia spotted James passing by the conference room. He paused in the doorway, taking in the goal-filled whiteboard with a small smile of approval before continuing on his way.

Tomorrow, she would need to start addressing the specific issues plaguing the project - Dmitri's quality problems, the revised schedule for Elizabeth, the authentication system architecture. But today, she'd taken a critical first step in transforming a fragmented group into a cohesive team with shared purpose and direction.

✧ ✧ ✧

By Thursday morning, Marcia had transformed the team's initial input into a draft goals document. The exercise had energised her, giving shape to what had previously felt like an overwhelming tangle of problems. Now she needed to get the team's buy-in on the refined vision.

She'd booked the larger conference room and arrived early to set up. Instead of the traditional meeting arrangement, she pushed the tables against the walls and arranged chairs in a semicircle facing a blank whiteboard wall, with Post-it notes and markers at each seat. On a side table, she placed extra markers, sticky notes, and - remembering Mei's approach - a tray of pastries she'd picked up on her way in.

Victor arrived first, precisely at 9:30 am. He paused in the doorway, eyeing the unusual room arrangement with suspicion.

"We're doing something different today," Marcia explained before he could object. "More interactive."

Victor didn't look convinced but took a seat, carefully adjusting it to align perfectly with the others. Mei arrived next, her face brightening at the room setup.

"This looks fun," she said, helping herself to a pastry.

The teams best ideas always seemed to emerge from face-to-face discussions rather than digital exchanges. As team members filed in, several carried laptops - a reminder that despite being a technology company, many workflows still revolved around physical documentation and in-person collaboration.

Within minutes, the entire team had assembled, coffee cups and notepads in hand, curious expressions on their faces. Dmitri looked more rested than he had all week, while Thomas and Priya sat together, continuing a technical discussion from earlier.

"Thanks for making time for this," Marcia began, standing by the whiteboard. "Yesterday, we started an important conversation about our team goals. Today, we're going to dig deeper and get specific."

She handed out copies of the draft document she'd prepared. "This synthesises what everyone shared yesterday. It's not final - it's a starting point for today's discussion."

The team reviewed the document silently. Marcia had distilled their wide-ranging input into five core goals:

1. Deliver reliable, high-quality solutions that provide genuine value to users.
2. Build technically sound systems that can adapt to future needs.
3. Honour commitments through realistic planning and transparent communication.
4. Foster a collaborative environment where diverse expertise is respected.
5. Maintain sustainable pace that enables continuous growth and well-being.

"These all sound good on paper," Dmitri said, breaking the silence. "But how do they help us when priorities conflict? If meeting a commitment requires technical compromise, which takes precedence?"

"That's exactly the conversation we need to have," Marcia replied. "These goals aren't just nice statements to hang on the wall. They're decision-making tools for exactly those tough situations."

She turned to the whiteboard and wrote "PRIORITISATION" in large letters.

"Let's talk through some real scenarios the team has faced and see how these goals would guide our decisions."

For the next thirty minutes, the team discussed specific challenges they'd encountered: the authentication system debate, the quality issues in Dmitri's components, the changing specifications from business stakeholders.

As they talked, Marcia noted how team members naturally gravitated toward different goals. Victor consistently emphasised quality and technical soundness. Dmitri focused on honouring commitments. Mei advocated for collaboration and sustainability.

"I see a pattern emerging," Marcia observed. "We all value these goals, but we weight them differently based on our roles and perspectives. What if we explicitly prioritised them?"

She drew a simple matrix on the whiteboard with the five goals listed down the left side. "Let's each rank these from 1 to 5, with 1 being most important to you personally."

The exercise revealed telling patterns. Technical team members like Victor ranked quality and technical soundness highest. Dmitri and Priya prioritised honouring commitments. Mei emphasised collaboration and sustainability.

"This explains so much about our previous conflicts," Thomas observed. "We've been operating with different internal priority lists."

"Exactly," Marcia agreed. "And there's no single 'right' prioritisation. Different situations might call for different priorities. But we need a shared team understanding of what typically comes first."

She turned to a fresh section of the whiteboard. "Now, as a team, let's create our official priority order. This isn't about individual preferences anymore - it's about what will make us most successful as a group."

The discussion that followed was animated but remarkably constructive. Victor advocated passionately for quality as the top priority: "If we deliver poor quality, nothing else matters in the long run."

Dmitri countered that honouring commitments had to come first: "Without client trust, we won't have the opportunity to demonstrate quality."

Mei suggested that sustainable pace might be foundational: "We can't maintain quality or honour commitments if we're burning out."

What struck Marcia most was how the team members engaged with each other directly rather than speaking through her. They were challenging each other's perspectives but with growing respect for the different viewpoints.

Jason, who had been relatively quiet until now, made an observation that shifted the conversation: "What if we're thinking about this wrong? Maybe it's not a simple rank order but a hierarchy where some goals enable others."

He approached the whiteboard and sketched a simple pyramid. "Sustainable pace creates the foundation for everything else. Collaboration enables quality work and technical soundness. Those technical aspects allow us to honour our commitments to clients."

The team fell silent, considering this framework.

"That... actually makes sense," Victor said, sounding mildly surprised.

"It aligns with what we're experiencing," Dmitri agreed. "When we sacrificed sustainable pace, quality suffered. When quality suffered, we couldn't honour our commitments."

Marcia watched with growing satisfaction as the team refined Jason's model, discussing the interconnections between goals and eventually creating a more nuanced framework than a simple ranked list.

"This is excellent," she said when they'd reached consensus. "Now let's test it against our current challenges. How would this framework guide our decision about the authentication system?"

The team walked through the scenario step by step, applying their newly articulated goals. The resulting approach was balanced: implement Victor's robust solution but with Dmitri's phased timeline, maintaining quality without creating unsustainable pressure.

"And what about our response to changing business requirements?" Marcia asked.

Again, the team applied their framework, arriving at a more collaborative approach than they'd used previously - one that respected the business needs while being transparent about technical implications.

As the meeting neared its end, Marcia saw something she hadn't observed before: genuine alignment. Team members were nodding as others spoke, building on each other's ideas rather than talking past one another.

"We've made tremendous progress today," she said, taking photos of the whiteboard. "I'll document our agreed framework and circulate it by tomorrow morning. This will guide how we approach our revised project plan for Elizabeth tomorrow."

As the team gathered their things, conversations continued organically, with Victor and Dmitri actually discussing a technical approach without their usual tension. Mei caught Marcia's eye and gave a subtle thumbs-up.

"One last thing," Marcia added as people headed toward the door. "This goals framework isn't just for big decisions. I'd like us to reference it explicitly in our daily stand-ups and team meetings. It should become part of our shared language."

Marcia reflected on the session with growing optimism. The team had shown not just cooperation but genuine engagement with building a shared vision. They weren't just following her lead - they were actively contributing to creating something meaningful together.

She began drafting the formal goals document, incorporating the hierarchical model Jason had proposed and the specific examples they'd discussed. This wasn't a theoretical exercise anymore but a practical tool the team had built together.

A calendar notification popped up on her screen: "Elizabeth Parker - Status Update" in fifteen minutes. Marcia gathered her notes, knowing Elizabeth would want concrete progress on the revised schedule. She didn't have that yet - but she had something potentially more valuable: a framework for making and communicating decisions that would allow them to deliver what truly mattered.

As she headed to the call, Marcia spotted the team gathered around Dmitri's workstation, whiteboard markers in hand, sketching what looked like a component diagram. They were already applying their new approach to a technical challenge without waiting for her direction.

Marcia felt like she was witnessing the emergence of a true team - not just a collection of talented individuals, but a unified group with shared vision and goals.

✧　✧　✧

Friday morning arrived with a sense of anticipation. Marcia had spent the previous evening finalising the team goals document, incorporating the collaborative framework they'd developed together. Now, as team members settled at their desks, she sent the email they'd been waiting for:

Subject: Draft Team Goals Framework - Please Review

Within minutes, she noticed the team opening the document, some leaning toward their screens with focused attention, others scrolling thoughtfully through the pages. Victor printed a copy immediately, making careful annotations with a red pen. Mei read it with a small smile, occasionally glancing toward other team members to gauge their reactions.

Marcia had put significant thought into the document's structure. Instead of a simple bullet list, she'd created a visual representation of the hierarchical model Jason had proposed, showing how each goal supported the others. She'd included specific examples of how these principles would guide decision-making in various scenarios the team had actually faced.

A soft vibration from her bag signalled a text, it was from James: *Saw the goals framework. Impressive work in such a short time. How's the team responding?*

She typed back: *Reviewing now. Holding my breath.*

James replied with a simple thumbs-up emoji.

As Marcia checked her email for the final version of the revised schedule they'd be sending to Elizabeth today, a message notification appeared in the corner of her screen:

Victor Kowalski: Re: Draft Team Goals Framework

She clicked it open, bracing herself for a list of technical critiques.

Marcia,

The framework accurately represents our discussions and provides clear guidance for decision-making. I particularly appreciate the explicit recognition that technical excellence supports our ability to honour commitments, rather than competing with it.

One suggestion: Consider adding a section on how we will measure progress against these goals. Without measurement, it's difficult to determine if we're improving.

- Victor

Marcia blinked in surprise. Not only was Victor's feedback positive, but his suggestion was constructive and entirely reasonable. She quickly replied, thanking him for the input and agreeing to incorporate a measurement section.

Over the next hour, responses trickled in from other team members. Dmitri noted the framework would help manage client expectations more effectively. Mei highlighted the collaborative way the document had been created as evidence they were already putting the principles into practice. Thomas appreciated the clarity about quality standards.

By mid-morning, Marcia had incorporated their feedback and finalised the document. The positive responses gave her confidence to move forward with the next step - making this more than just a document but a visible commitment.

"I need your help with something," she said, approaching Mei at her desk. "Do you have a few minutes?"

Fifteen minutes later, they returned to the Enterprise Solutions area rolling a large blank poster board mounted on an easel. Marcia set it up at the entrance to their team space, visible to everyone walking by.

"Team meeting in five minutes," she announced. "Just a quick one."

The team gathered around the poster board with curious expressions. Marcia handed out coloured markers to each person.

"We've created something important together," she began. "This isn't just my vision or management's mandate. It's our collective agreement about what matters most to us as a team."

She tapped the large blank poster. "I'd like us all to transfer our framework to this board and sign it - not because it's a contract, but because it represents our shared commitment to how we'll work together."

Mei immediately stepped forward, taking a blue marker. "I'll start with the foundation." She began drawing the hierarchical pyramid they'd developed, adding "Sustainable Pace" at the base. One by one, team members added elements to the visual representation, each contributing in their own style.

Victor meticulously drew the technical excellence section, adding precise bulleted standards he would champion. Dmitri mapped out how they'd approach honouring commitments. Thomas detailed quality assurance practices. Priya added notes about stakeholder collaboration. Jason incorporated user-centred principles.

When they finished, the poster displayed not just a generic framework but a richly detailed map of how their team specifically would approach their work - what they valued, how they'd make decisions, and how they'd resolve conflicts.

Importantly, the visuals and the team engagement made it all more memorable.

"Now, let's make it official," Marcia said, offering a black marker. "Who wants to be first?"

To everyone's surprise, Victor stepped forward. "Since I was the most sceptical initially, it seems appropriate that I demonstrate my commitment now." He signed his name in neat, precise letters at the bottom of the poster.

One by one, each team member added their signature. Marcia signed last, adding the current date beneath her name.

"I'm going to hang this where we can all see it," she said. "Not as decoration, but as a daily reminder of what we've agreed matters most."

As she secured the poster to the wall near their team area, Marcia noticed James walking by with Robert Miller. The company founder paused, studying the poster and the team gathered around it.

"Impressive," Miller remarked to James, just loud enough for Marcia to overhear. "From crisis to cohesion in less than a week."

James caught Marcia's eye and gave her another nod of approval before continuing down the hallway with Miller.

When the team dispersed back to their desks, Marcia noticed something different in their interactions. Victor stopped by Dmitri's desk to discuss an approach rather than sending a critical email. Mei was showing Thomas something on her screen, their conversation animated and productive. Even Priya, who had been somewhat peripheral to the team dynamics, was more engaged, walking through requirement updates with Jason.

Later that afternoon, as Marcia finalised the revised project schedule for Elizabeth, she incorporated direct references to the team goals framework, showing how their decisions aligned with their core principles. She explained that the extended timeline wasn't just a delayed delivery but a deliberate choice to honour their commitment to quality and sustainability.

To her surprise, Elizabeth's response was more positive than expected:

Marcia,

The revised schedule shows thoughtful planning rather than arbitrary delays. I appreciate your team's framework - it helps me understand the reasoning behind your approach and gives me confidence you're making decisions based on consistent principles rather than convenience.

Let's proceed with this plan. I'll update our stakeholders accordingly.

Thanks, Elizabeth

As the workday wound down, Marcia took a moment to update her leadership notebook, reflecting on the week's transformation. They still faced significant technical challenges with the FreshWorks project. Quality issues remained to be resolved. The timeline was tight even with the extension.

But something fundamental had shifted. The team now had a shared language for discussing priorities and making decisions. They had explicit permission to value sustainability alongside delivery. Most importantly, they had begun to see themselves as a unified team with a common purpose rather than individual contributors with competing agendas.

Marcia closed her notebook - the same one she'd started with on day one, now transformed from a debugging log into something else entirely. The early pages still showed system diagrams and error codes. But the recent pages mapped human patterns, team dynamics, individual strengths. She'd been debugging people systems without realising it.

Her phone vibrated with a calendar invitation from Mei: *Team lunch - celebrating our new framework - Monday 12:30 pm. Potluck - bring a dish to share.* All team members were already marked as attending.

Marcia accepted with a smile. This wasn't her initiative - it was organic team building emerging naturally from their new sense of shared identity.

As she packed up for the weekend, Marcia paused to look at the signed poster. It wasn't perfect - no framework could be. They would likely need to revise it as they learned and grew together. But it was an authentic representation of what this specific team valued and how they wanted to work together.

James stopped by her desk on his way out. "Congratulations," he said simply.

"We still have a long way to go," Marcia replied. "The technical challenges haven't disappeared, and we're still behind schedule even with the extension."

"True," James acknowledged. "But now you're facing those challenges as a team rather than a collection of individuals. That makes all the difference."

He tapped the Team Leaders Toolbox folder sitting on her desk. "You've established the foundation. Next week, you can start building on it - mapping skills, allocating resources, creating a roadmap."

Marcia nodded, already thinking about the next steps. "One tool at a time."

"Exactly," James said with a smile. "Leadership isn't about solving every problem at once. It's about building the systems that enable the team to solve problems together."

As James left, Marcia took one final look at the team area before heading out. The signed goals poster stood as a visible symbol of the transformation that had begun - not just a document or a management exercise, but the beginning of a new team identity built on shared purpose and mutual respect.

The technical challenges of the FreshWorks project remained daunting, but Marcia felt genuinely confident that they would face those challenges together - as a true team.

Chapter 5
Taking Inventory

Monday morning brought new energy to the Enterprise Solutions team. The team goals framework hanging prominently on the wall seemed to have catalysed something - a subtle shift in how team members interacted. People were discussing issues face-to-face rather than through terse emails. Even Victor had removed his headphones a few times to engage directly with colleagues.

Marcia sipped her coffee, observing these positive signs from her desk. The crisis with Elizabeth had been temporarily averted thanks to the revised schedule, but substantial challenges remained. The authentication system still needed redesign, Dmitri's components required quality improvements, and overall progress remained slower than ideal.

She opened the Team Leaders Toolbox folder James had given her, turning to the next section: "Skills Matrix." The concept was straightforward - create a grid mapping team members against required skills to understand strengths and gaps. It seemed like precisely what she needed to optimise how work was assigned.

As she considered how to introduce this tool, Marcia noticed something happening across the office space. Victor was attempting to help Priya with what appeared to be a database issue, but their conversation looked increasingly frustrated. Victor's hands moved rapidly as he tried to explain something technical while Priya nodded with a confused expression.

Meanwhile, Jason was working independently on a UI component that Mei had mentioned having experience with. And Thomas sat waiting for components to test, though Dmitri appeared to be starting work on new features rather than fixing the quality issues Thomas had identified.

"They're all working hard, but not necessarily on the right things," Marcia murmured to herself.

She made her way to Victor's desk just as Priya was walking away, shoulders slumped in frustration.

"Everything okay?" Marcia asked.

Victor sighed. "Priya is struggling with a database query that's affecting her module. I tried to explain the proper approach, but..." he trailed off, gesturing vaguely.

"But database queries aren't her primary skill set," Marcia finished for him.

"Precisely. She's an excellent front-end developer, but database optimisation requires different expertise."

Marcia nodded. "And would this be a quick task for you or Dmitri?"

"Twenty minutes, perhaps thirty," Victor replied. "For Priya, it might take days of trial and error, with suboptimal results."

"I see," Marcia said thoughtfully. "What about the authentication module you're working on now? Could anyone else on the team handle that?"

Victor considered this. "Portions of it, perhaps. Mei has worked with similar systems before."

This confirmed what Marcia was beginning to suspect - they were allocating work based on project modules rather than skill alignment. The result was experts struggling with unfamiliar tasks while their specialised knowledge remained untapped where it would be most valuable.

She continued her observations, stopping by Jason's desk next.

"That UI component looks familiar," she commented, looking at his screen.

Jason nodded. "It's for the inventory section. I'm trying to implement this dropdown with nested categorisation, but it's getting complicated with the filtering requirements."

"Didn't Mei build something similar for the vendor portal last year?" Marcia asked.

Jason looked surprised. "Did she? I didn't know that."

At Thomas's workstation, the situation was equally telling. The QA analyst sat with a mostly empty test tracking sheet, occasionally running tests on components that had been delivered but mostly waiting.

"Not much to test yet?" Marcia asked.

Thomas shook his head. "Dmitri mentioned he's starting on the reporting feature today. But I still have all these defects logged from last week that haven't been addressed."

"So you're blocked on meaningful progress until those are fixed?"

"Essentially, yes," Thomas confirmed. "But everyone's so focused on new features that quality fixes keep getting deprioritised."

The pattern was clear: work was being assigned based on project areas rather than skills and dependencies. This created bottlenecks, quality issues, and inefficient use of everyone's abilities.

At her desk again, Marcia pulled out her notebook and sketched a quick matrix with team members down one side and key skills across the top. She briefly considered creating a digital version in Excel to share via email, but decided against it - the server-based file sharing system was notoriously slow, and the company's IT department was still months away from their planned cloud storage rollout. Instead, she'd create a physical version for the team area. She began filling in what she knew, but the gaps in her knowledge were glaring. She understood broad strengths, but not the nuanced skill levels that would allow for optimal work allocation.

Her email notification chimed again - twenty new messages since lunch, most requiring detailed responses that would eat into her afternoon.

The team lunch Mei had organised was scheduled for 12:30 pm. Afterwards would be a perfect opportunity to introduce the skills matrix concept in a collaborative setting.

Her phone rang - Elizabeth Parker calling for a status update.

"Marcia, I've been reviewing the revised schedule," Elizabeth said after brief pleasantries. "I'm cautiously optimistic about the overall approach, but I have concerns about the resource allocation. How confident are you that you have the right people assigned to the right components?"

The question couldn't have been more timely.

"Actually, Elizabeth, that's exactly what I'm working on today," Marcia replied. "I've noticed some inefficiencies in how we're distributing work. We're going to be implementing a more systematic approach to match tasks with skills."

"That sounds promising," Elizabeth said, her tone warming slightly. "What specifically are you changing?"

"We've been organising work by module or feature, which means sometimes people are working outside their areas of expertise," Marcia explained. "I'm creating a skills inventory to ensure we leverage everyone's strengths more effectively."

"Smart approach," Elizabeth commented. "When can I see how this affects the critical path timelines?"

"I should have an updated resource allocation plan by our next call," Marcia promised. "Once we properly align skills with tasks, I expect we'll see significant efficiency improvements."

After finishing the call, Marcia reviewed the skills matrix template from James's toolkit again. This wasn't just about documenting capabilities - it was about uncovering hidden strengths, addressing gaps, and fundamentally changing how work flowed through the team.

As lunchtime approached, she printed blank matrix templates for everyone, ready to begin the next phase of transforming her group into a high-performing team.

✧ ✧ ✧

The conference room transformed into an impromptu dining area as team members filed in, each carrying a dish for the potluck. Mei had suggested the idea - a 'bring a dish to share' lunch to celebrate recent progress - and the response had been surprisingly enthusiastic.

Marcia smiled as she surveyed the spread forming on the side table. Mei, ever the thoughtful connector, brought homemade dumplings with neatly labelled dipping sauces. Victor contributed an orderly stack of chicken-mayo sandwiches layered with Mrs. Ball's Chutney - each one diagonally sliced and wrapped in parchment with near-mathematical precision. Beside them, he placed a small paper bag filled with biltong strips and a handwritten label: *"For the curious - try with caution."* Dmitri arrived with a large glass bowl of Olivier salad - a Russian classic of finely chopped potatoes, eggs, pickles, and peas, dressed generously in mayonnaise and garnished with dill.

Jason, embracing the casual vibe, brought a bag of fancy chips and a tub of guacamole he'd picked up on the way in. Priya laid down a warm container of spiced vegetable pulao, fragrant with cardamom and cloves. Thomas, ever efficient, brought supermarket mini quiches, still in their packaging but warmed and ready.

Marcia had brought store-bought brownies, still in their plastic tray, with a sticky note that read *"They're better than they look."*

The relaxed mood carried through to the seating arrangement. Dmitri sat beside Victor rather than across from him, and Jason had chosen a seat next to Thomas, with whom he rarely interacted. Conversation flowed easily - less about bugs and deadlines, more about recipes, weekend plans, and the joy of real food that didn't come from the vending machine.

"Thanks for organising this, Mei," Marcia said as she settled into her chair. "It's exactly what we needed after last week's intensity."

Mei beamed. "I thought we should celebrate our progress with the team goals. Plus, food always makes conversations easier."

Conversation flowed naturally for the first twenty-five minutes - weekend activities, a new coffee shop that had opened nearby, and good-natured complaints about Seattle's persistent haze. Marcia observed the interactions with interest, noting how much more comfortable everyone seemed in this setting - relaxed, laughing, and connecting in ways that rarely happened during standard meetings.

As the meal began to wind down and people reached for second cups of coffee or began stacking empty containers, Marcia stood and gently tapped her glass with a spoon. "Before everyone disappears - would you be open to doing a short team activity once we've cleared up?"

There were a few curious glances and nods of agreement.

"It's something light but useful," she added. "I think you'll find it interesting - and it won't take long."

With a shared sense of purpose, the team began clearing plates, stacking leftover food, and wiping down the tables. A few minutes later, they returned to the room, pulling chairs back into a loose semicircle.

Marcia stepped to the front and pulled out the blank templates she'd prepared. "Thanks for sticking around. While we're all together, I want to share something I noticed this morning," she began. "We have incredible talent on this team, but I'm not sure we're using everyone's strengths as effectively as we could."

She passed out the templates. "This is called a skills matrix. It's a simple tool to help us understand who has what capabilities - and at what level."

Victor studied the paper with his characteristic intensity. "This seems logical. Proper resource allocation should be based on objectively measured capabilities."

"Exactly," Marcia nodded. "But there's an important distinction - this isn't about performance evaluation. It's about self-assessment and team awareness."

Dmitri looked sceptical. "And how is this different from typical performance reviews?"

"In three key ways," Marcia explained. "First, it's self-rated rather than manager-rated. You know your skills better than anyone. Second, it's transparent to the whole team, so everyone knows who to go to for specific expertise. And third, it's not about judging - it's about matching the right people to the right tasks."

"I like that approach," Mei said, already scanning the skill categories. "But I notice some important capabilities aren't listed here."

"This is just a starting template," Marcia clarified. "Before we fill it out, I'd like us to customise it for our specific needs. What skills are critical for our work that should be included?"

The team enthusiastically jumped in. Victor suggested multiple technical categories - database optimisation, security protocols, system architecture. Mei added soft skills like stakeholder communication and requirements analysis. Thomas contributed testing methodologies and quality assurance frameworks.

Marcia captured their suggestions, occasionally consolidating similar items, until they had a comprehensive list that reflected the full range of capabilities required for their work.

"Now comes the self-assessment part," she explained, drawing a simple rating scale on the whiteboard. "For each skill, rate yourself from one to five, with one meaning basic familiarity and five meaning expert-level mastery. Be honest - this isn't about impressing anyone but about understanding our collective capabilities."

"What if I don't know a skill at all?" Jason asked.

"Leave it blank," Marcia replied. "That's valuable information too."

The room fell quiet as everyone focused on their assessments. Marcia watched with interest as team members occasionally paused, deep in thought over particular ratings. Victor seemed to hold himself to extremely high standards, rarely giving himself the highest rating despite his evident expertise. Mei appeared hesitant when rating technical skills but confident with interpersonal ones.

After about fifteen minutes, Priya looked up from her completed matrix. "This is enlightening. I knew I was stronger in front-end development, but seeing everything mapped out makes it clearer where I could contribute more effectively."

"That's exactly the point," Marcia said. "Would anyone be willing to share something they discovered while doing this exercise?"

Jason raised his hand. "I realised I have experience with the charting library we're using, but I don't think anyone knows that since I joined after that component was assigned."

"I've been struggling with those charts," Dmitri admitted, a rare request for help as he began to feel safer in his team environment. "Perhaps we should discuss collaboration."

Thomas spoke next. "I rated myself highly in automated testing frameworks, but we haven't implemented many on this project. It could significantly improve our quality verification process."

One by one, team members shared insights - hidden skills, untapped experiences, and interests in developing new capabilities. The energy in the room shifted as people recognised opportunities to both contribute more effectively and potentially grow in new directions.

"So what happens next?" Victor asked pragmatically. "We have this information, but how do we apply it?"

"First, I'll compile everyone's self-assessments into a master matrix that we'll share with the whole team," Marcia explained. "Then we'll use it to inform how we allocate tasks going forward."

She stepped up to a blank whiteboard. "Let me give you a concrete example from this morning. Priya was struggling with database queries that would take Victor or Dmitri a fraction of the time to complete. Meanwhile, Victor was working on authentication that Mei has relevant experience with."

She sketched a quick diagram showing current versus potential task allocation. "If we reallocated based on skills, we could significantly improve both efficiency and quality."

"But wouldn't that disrupt our current module ownership?" Dmitri asked. "Each person has been responsible for specific components."

"That's a fair concern," Marcia acknowledged. "I'm not suggesting we completely abandon module ownership, but rather that we become more flexible about who does what within our overall structure. Perhaps we keep primary responsibility for modules but leverage specific skills across boundaries when it makes sense."

The team discussed the implications of this approach - the advantages in efficiency, the potential challenges in coordination, the opportunities for knowledge sharing and skill development.

As the activity concluded, Marcia collected the completed self-assessments. "I'll compile these and share the results tomorrow. Then we can discuss how to apply this knowledge to our current workload."

The team dispersed back to their desks with a new energy. Marcia noticed Priya approaching Victor, likely about that database query issue. Nearby, Jason and Dmitri were already discussing the charting component. The matrix exercise had catalysed conversations that might not have happened otherwise.

Returning to her desk, Marcia began entering the self-assessments into a spreadsheet. The patterns were fascinating - areas of collective strength, surprising gaps, and complementary skills that could be better leveraged. This wasn't just about documenting capabilities; it was about seeing the team as an interconnected system rather than isolated contributors.

James made his way over, glancing at her work. "Skills matrix? Moving right along through the toolkit, I see."

"It was exactly what we needed," Marcia replied. "I've been assigning work based on what I thought people could do, not what they actually excel at."

"That's the usual leadership trap," James smiled. "We make assumptions instead of asking directly. How did the team respond?"

"Better than I expected. They were honest about both strengths and limitations. Even Victor participated wholeheartedly."

"Excellent," James nodded. "Just remember - once you have this information, the real work begins. Using it effectively to reassign responsibilities can be delicate."

As James walked away, Marcia considered his warning. The matrix had revealed valuable insights, but translating that knowledge into changed work patterns would require careful handling. People naturally became attached to their assigned responsibilities, and shifting those boundaries could create resistance.

She returned to her spreadsheet, already planning how to approach the next critical step: creating a resource allocation plan that would optimise the team's collective skills while respecting individual ownership and development goals.

Author's Note

In practice, the team will fill in each of their ratings, and after a few days once the whole team has done a first pass, it would be normal for people to adjust their skill ratings relative to each other. Also, over time, people will develop new skills, increase their rating in existing skills, and perhaps get rusty and reduce a skill rating. The team should be encouraged to treat the skills matrix as a living document and update it as needed.

Later, we will see how the skills matrix can provide input into training plans and help develop organisational capability.

Lastly, I recommend you do not use the skills matrix as part of the annual review process as this will undermine the teams willingness to use it as a transparent and shared tool.

✧ ✧ ✧

By Tuesday afternoon, Marcia had transformed the team's individual assessments into a comprehensive skills matrix. The colourful spreadsheet revealed patterns that weren't immediately obvious from their day-to-day interactions. She printed a large version and pinned it to the wall next to their team goals poster, then sent a meeting invitation for a quick team huddle.

"This is fascinating," Mei said as the team gathered around the matrix. "I had no idea Jason was so strong in UX design."

Jason shrugged modestly. "I took some specialised courses before joining Alpha."

"And Thomas, I didn't realise you had experience with automated testing frameworks," Victor noted, studying the chart with interest. "We should be leveraging that expertise."

Thomas nodded. "I've been wanting to implement more automation, but wasn't sure how to bring it up."

Marcia let them explore the matrix for a few minutes, watching as they discovered new things about each other's capabilities. The energy was positive - people seemed genuinely interested rather than competitive or defensive.

"So what exactly do we do with this information?" Dmitri finally asked. "It's interesting, but how does it change our approach to the FreshWorks project?"

"That's the million-dollar question," Marcia replied. "I've been thinking about that since yesterday." She moved to the whiteboard and sketched a simple diagram. "Currently, we assign work like this - by module or feature. Victor owns authentication, Dmitri handles database components, and so on."

She drew a different structure beside it. "But what if we organised around skills instead? What if we temporarily reassigned certain tasks based on who could complete them most efficiently?"

"You mean like having me help with Priya's database queries?" Victor asked.

"Exactly. Or having Jason and Mei collaborate on UI components since they both have strong skills there. Or letting Thomas implement automated testing across all modules rather than each person handling their own testing approach."

The team fell silent, considering the implications.

"It would certainly be more efficient," Dmitri acknowledged. "But wouldn't it create coordination problems? If multiple people work on a single module, who has final responsibility?"

"That's a valid concern," Marcia agreed. "I'm not suggesting we completely abandon module ownership. The module owner would still have final integration responsibility and architectural decisions. But specific tasks within the module could be allocated based on who has the right skills."

"I see potential benefits," Victor said thoughtfully. "For instance, the database queries in Priya's module are causing performance issues that affect the entire system. If I could resolve those quickly, everyone would benefit."

"And I could help Victor with some of the UI elements in the authentication module," Mei offered. "That would free him to focus on the security protocols where his expertise is most valuable."

Priya, who had been quiet until now, spoke up. "I've been struggling with those database queries for days. If Victor could handle them, I could focus on the user interaction flow where I'm more effective."

One by one, team members began identifying potential task exchanges that could leverage their respective strengths. Marcia captured these on the whiteboard, creating a rough outline of a new allocation approach.

"This looks promising," she said when they'd exhausted their initial ideas. "But before we implement any changes, I want to run an experiment. Let's try just two or three of these reassignments first and see how they work in practice."

She circled three items on the whiteboard:

1. Victor takes over database optimisation in Priya's module.
2. Thomas implements automated testing framework for critical components.
3. Jason and Mei collaborate on charting components.

"These are discrete tasks with clear boundaries, making them good candidates for our experiment," Marcia explained. "We'll try them for the rest of this week, then evaluate results on Friday."

"Will this impact our timeline?" Dmitri asked, ever focused on delivery commitments.

"If our hypothesis is correct, it should actually accelerate progress," Marcia replied. "But that's why we're testing it before making broader changes."

They dedicated the next twenty minutes working out the specifics of each reassignment - what exactly would be transferred, how handoffs would work, and how they'd measure success.

"One last thing," Marcia added as they wrapped up. "This isn't just about short-term efficiency. It's also about knowledge sharing. When you're working in someone else's domain, document what you're doing so they can learn from your approach."

The team dispersed with a renewed sense of purpose. Marcia watched as Victor immediately went to Priya's desk to discuss the database issues, while Jason approached Mei about the charting components. The matrix had catalysed not just task reassignment but also new conversations and connections.

Later that afternoon, Marcia checked in with each pair to see how the transitions were progressing. The results were encouraging. Victor had already identified the root cause of Priya's database performance issues - a nested query that could be substantially optimised. Thomas was setting up a testing framework that would automatically verify key components, potentially catching defects much earlier. And Jason and Mei were sketching a unified approach to charts that would improve both functionality and appearance.

As Marcia updated her project tracking sheet, she noticed something remarkable - their velocity estimates had improved significantly just from these three reassignments. If the experiment proved successful, broader application of this approach could potentially bring them back on schedule without the quality compromises that had plagued them before.

Her phone buzzed with a text from James: *How's the skills matrix implementation going?*

She replied. *First experiments underway. Early signs promising. Team engaged and collaborative.*

James texted back. *Excellent, Next challenge will be expanding without creating chaos. Balance is key.*

Marcia pondered his words as she reviewed the skills matrix again. The challenge ahead wasn't just technical but organisational - how to systematically leverage everyone's strengths without losing coherence and accountability. They needed a more formal resource allocation plan that maintained clear ownership while enabling flexible collaboration.

She opened a new document and began outlining a structured approach. The team's goals framework provided their "why" - the skills matrix had revealed their "who" and "what" - now they needed the "how" of resource allocation to bring it all together.

From her desk, Marcia could see Victor and Priya engaged in animated conversation, with Victor sketching something on a notepad while Priya nodded with growing understanding. Nearby, Thomas was demonstrating something to Dmitri, who appeared genuinely interested rather than his usual stoic self. These collaborative interactions - rare before the skills matrix - suggested they were moving in the right direction.

The skills matrix had accomplished something important beyond just efficiency - it had created a foundation for mutual respect based on recognising each person's unique value to the team. That recognition was already changing how they interacted, transforming competition into collaboration and isolation into engagement.

Now the challenge was to formalise this approach into a sustainable system that would carry them through the FreshWorks project and beyond.

✦ ✦ ✦

Victor stood back from Priya's monitor, arms crossed but with a hint of satisfaction on his face that Marcia hadn't seen before.

For once the problem matched the precision of his thinking, and the knot of tension in his shoulders eased. Solving nested-query performance, he realised, was easier than untangling human variables - and immeasurably calmer.

"Try it now," he said.

Priya ran the query that had been plaguing her for days. The results appeared almost instantly - a dramatic improvement from the thirty-second wait time they'd been experiencing.

"That's incredible!" Priya exclaimed. "What exactly did you change?"

Victor launched into an explanation of nested queries and index optimisation that would have been indecipherable to most, but Priya followed along, asking thoughtful questions. Marcia observed from nearby, noting how Victor seemed genuinely pleased to share his expertise.

"I've documented the approach," Victor added, sending Priya an email. "The same principles can be applied to similar queries throughout your module."

"This will save me hours of frustration," Priya said. "Thank you."

It had been three days since they'd implemented the experimental task reassignments, and Marcia was witnessing similar successes throughout the team. Thomas had established an automated testing framework that caught three critical bugs before they could affect other components. Mei and Jason had collaborated on a unified charting approach that would provide consistent visualisation across the entire application.

The team's morning stand-up meeting had a different energy - more collaborative updates, offers of assistance, and genuine interest in each other's work. Even Elizabeth had noticed the change during their Wednesday status call, commenting on the improved quality metrics and accelerated progress on previously stalled components.

"Marcia, got a minute?" Dmitri approached her desk, tablet in hand.

"Of course. How are things progressing with the reporting module?"

"That's what I wanted to discuss." Dmitri pulled up a chair. "After seeing the results of our experiment, I've been thinking about other potential reassignments."

This was unexpected - Dmitri had been the most cautious about changing their approach.

"I'm listening," Marcia encouraged.

"The reporting module has complex data transformation requirements," Dmitri explained. "It's taking me significant time to get right. But I noticed on the skills matrix that Jason has strong data transformation experience."

"He does," Marcia confirmed.

"Meanwhile, I see he's working on user preferences that involve complex state management, which happens to be one of my strengths." Dmitri pulled up both components on his tablet. "I believe if we exchanged these specific tasks, we could both work more efficiently."

Marcia couldn't help but smile. This was exactly the kind of self-organisation she'd hoped the skills matrix would eventually encourage.

"That sounds like a great idea. Have you discussed it with Jason yet?"

"Briefly this morning. He seemed receptive but suggested I speak with you first since it goes beyond our initial experiment."

"I appreciate that," Marcia said. "But this is exactly the kind of collaboration I was hoping for. If you and Jason both agree it makes sense, you have my full support."

As Dmitri returned to his desk, Marcia reflected on how quickly the dynamic had shifted. The skills matrix had transformed from a management tool into a catalyst for team-led collaboration. People were beginning to identify opportunities themselves rather than waiting for her direction.

By Friday afternoon, it was time to evaluate their experiment. Marcia gathered the team in the conference room, where she'd prepared a simple dashboard showing their progress metrics before and after the reassignments.

"The results speak for themselves," she began, displaying the first chart. "Component completion rate has increased by 32% for the affected modules."

The second chart showed quality metrics. "Defect density has decreased by 47%, largely due to Thomas's automated testing framework catching issues earlier."

"And most importantly," she continued, switching to the third chart, "team member satisfaction has improved across the board." This data came from a quick pulse survey she'd asked everyone to complete that morning.

"It's clear our experiment has been successful," Marcia concluded. "The question now is how we expand this approach without creating confusion about ownership and accountability."

"I've been thinking about that," Victor surprised everyone by speaking up first. "What if we formalised a distinction between module ownership and task execution?"

"Go on," Marcia encouraged.

"The module owner would maintain architectural responsibility and final integration authority," Victor explained, warming to his topic. "But specific tasks within the module could be assigned based on the skills matrix to whoever has the most relevant expertise."

"That makes sense," Mei agreed. "It maintains clear accountability while allowing flexibility in how we get things done."

"We'd need a system to track these cross-module assignments," Thomas added pragmatically. "Our current project tool isn't set up for that."

"What if we used a simple board?" Jason suggested, moving to the whiteboard. He quickly sketched a grid with team members across the top and key project components down the side. "We could use different coloured markers to indicate ownership versus task contribution."

The team built on Jason's idea, collaboratively developing a visual system to track their new working approach. Marcia stepped back, letting them work through the details together - another positive sign of their evolving team dynamic.

"I think we've got something workable here," Marcia said when they'd finished. "Let's implement this tracking system and expand our skills-based assignments to the entire project starting Monday."

As the meeting wrapped up, Dmitri lingered behind. "This approach is very different from how I've worked before," he admitted. "In my previous positions, staying strictly in your lane was... expected."

"Change can be uncomfortable," Marcia acknowledged. "Is there something specific that concerns you?"

"Not concerns, exactly." Dmitri seemed to be choosing his words carefully. "But I wonder if I could take on a more formal role in helping coordinate these cross-module assignments? With my background in database work, I see many of the integration points."

Marcia considered this thoughtfully. Dmitri had been the team member most affected by the previous unsustainable workload. His request suggested he was not only embracing the new approach but wanted to help ensure its success.

"That's an excellent idea," she replied. "Would you be willing to draft a process for how we coordinate these assignments and present it to the team on Monday?"

Dmitri straightened slightly, a hint of pride in his posture. "I would be happy to."

Back in front of her monitor, Marcia updated her project dashboard with the latest metrics. The improvements were substantial enough that they might actually meet Elizabeth's revised timeline without the quality compromises that had caused problems before.

James swung by Marcia's desk, easily noticing the dashboard metrics on her screen. "Those are impressive numbers. The skills matrix experiment worked, I take it?"

"It went surprisingly well," Marcia replied. "The team has not only accepted the approach but is now extending it themselves. Dmitri is even taking on a coordination role."

"That's the real win," James nodded approvingly. "When the team starts driving the changes themselves, you know you're on the right track."

"We still have a long way to go with the FreshWorks project," Marcia cautioned. "But for the first time, I feel like we have a systematic approach to leverage everyone's strengths instead of just hoping for the best."

"Exactly what the skills matrix is designed to do," James reminded her. "And speaking of systems, have you thought about formalising your resource allocation approach next? The skills matrix tells you who can do what, but a resource allocation plan ensures everyone has sustainable workloads."

Marcia nodded, already thinking ahead to the next tool in the framework. The skills matrix had proven its value, but it was just one piece of the puzzle. They needed a comprehensive resource allocation plan to ensure their newly efficient team didn't fall back into unsustainable patterns.

"That's my focus for next week," she confirmed. "Now that we know who's best at what, we need to make sure they have the time and space to apply those skills effectively."

As she looked across the office, Marcia saw Victor helping Priya implement the database optimisation techniques he'd shown her. Nearby, Thomas was walking Jason through the automated testing framework. Mei and Dmitri were deep in conversation about reporting visualisations.

The skills matrix had done more than improve efficiency - it had transformed how the team saw each other, replacing competition with collaboration and isolation with connection. Individual strengths were becoming team assets rather than personal territories.

The FreshWorks project was beginning to feel less like a crisis and more like an opportunity to build something valuable together.

Nearly halfway through - how's your journey going?

If *Team Leaders Toolbox* has sparked some fresh thinking or helped you reflect on your leadership style so far, I'd love to hear what's landed for you.

A quick review helps others decide if this is the right book for them - and gives me insight into what's working, what's resonating, and what to keep improving.

To leave a review

▨ *Scan the QR code on this page*

💬 *Or head to your Amazon Orders page → find this book → and select "Write a Product Review"*

Real feedback builds better tools - just like in a team.
With gratitude,

Stephen J. McIntyre

Chapter 6
Work Visibility

"What do you mean we missed the authentication module deadline?" Marcia asked, trying to keep her voice level despite her surprise.

Victor shifted uncomfortably in his chair. "The core functionality is complete, but the integration with the user management system is still in progress. I thought we had until Friday."

It was Wednesday morning, and Elizabeth Parker had just emailed Marcia asking why the authentication module - scheduled for delivery to QA yesterday - hadn't appeared in the test environment.

"Our project plan clearly shows Tuesday as the delivery date," Marcia said, pulling up the schedule on her tablet. She turned it to show Victor the timeline with yesterday's date highlighted.

"I was working from this version," Victor countered, opening a document on his laptop. His schedule indeed showed Friday as the deadline.

Marcia frowned. "That's the old version from before our timeline revision. How are you tracking your tasks?"

"I maintain my own task list," Victor explained, showing her a meticulously organised spreadsheet. "I update it based on our planning meetings."

"And you?" Marcia asked, turning to Dmitri who had joined them.

"I use the company project management system," he replied. "But I only check it for my directly assigned tasks."

"What about you, Mei?" Marcia called across to the next desk.

Mei looked up from her computer. "I have a notebook where I write everything down during meetings. But sometimes I miss updates if I'm not in every discussion."

A pattern was emerging, and it wasn't good. Despite their progress with team goals and the skills matrix, they lacked a fundamental tool - a unified, visible system for tracking work and deadlines that everyone could access and trust.

"Let's pause here," Marcia said. "I need to respond to Elizabeth, then we should talk as a team."

Dropping into her chair, Marcia crafted a careful email to Elizabeth explaining the miscommunication and promising delivery by the end of day. Then she messaged James: *We've hit a workflow tracking issue. Any suggestions from the toolkit?*

His response came quickly: *Sounds like you need a visual task board. Physical beats digital for team visibility. Conference room B has a large mobile magnetic whiteboard that works well.*

Marcia grabbed her laptop and notebook, and headed to the supply room, returning with magnetic tape, colourful cards, and markers. She then used Outlook to reserve Conference Room B for an impromptu team meeting, watching as the room changed from white to blue in the shared calendar.

While several newer tech companies were experimenting with digital task boards and project management software, Alpha Consulting still operated primarily in the physical world.

A physical board that everyone could see and touch would create the immediate impact they needed.

Once everyone had assembled, Marcia got straight to the point.

"We have a visibility problem," she began directly. "This morning, we discovered that different team members are tracking their work in completely different systems - spreadsheets, notebooks, mental lists, outdated schedules. The result was a missed deadline that could have been avoided."

Nods around the table indicated no one could argue with this assessment.

"I propose we create a visual task board," Marcia continued, gesturing to the supplies she'd gathered. "A single source of truth that everyone can see and update."

"Like a Kanban board?" Thomas asked. "I used that in my previous role."

"Exactly," Marcia confirmed. "We'll create columns for different stages of work - To Do, In Progress, Review, and Done. Each task gets a card that moves across the board as work progresses."

"That seems unnecessarily manual," Victor commented. "We have digital tools for project management."

"The physical aspect is actually the point," Marcia explained. "Digital tools are easy to ignore or forget to check. A big visible board that we walk past every day is harder to miss. Think of it as the difference between having your alarm clock across the room versus next to your bed - which one forces you to actually get up?"

This analogy seemed to resonate with Victor, who nodded thoughtfully.

"What about remote work days?" Dmitri asked. "How would we update it if we're not in the office?"

"Good question," Marcia acknowledged. "We'll need a designated person to update the physical board based on our daily stand-up calls when someone is remote. And we can take a photo of the board to share after any changes."

For the next thirty minutes, the team worked together to create their task board, identifying current tasks and writing them on cards. Marcia noticed how the physical act of handling cards and placing them on the board created a different kind of engagement than typing into a digital system.

"Let's colour-code by component," Jason suggested, already organising cards by hue.

"And we should add due dates prominently on each card," Thomas added, writing dates in red marker.

Mei picked up a green marker. "What if we indicate dependencies between tasks with arrows? So we can see what's blocking what?"

The board quickly took shape as a colourful, information-rich display of their project status. When they stepped back to review it, something important became immediately apparent.

"We have way too many things in progress simultaneously," Marcia observed, pointing to the crowded middle column. "No wonder we're missing deadlines - we're spread too thin."

"And look at these dependencies," Dmitri added, tracing the green arrows between cards. "These three tasks are blocked waiting for the same component, but it's not even in progress yet."

The visual nature of the board revealed patterns that hadn't been visible in their disparate tracking systems. Work was piling up at certain stages, critical dependencies weren't being prioritised, and some team members had too many concurrent tasks.

"This is enlightening," Victor admitted, studying the board. "I can see three optimisation tasks I should prioritise that would unblock other work."

As they continued discussing the board, Marcia noticed something else - the team was naturally starting to reorder priorities and reassign tasks based on what they could now clearly see. The board wasn't just tracking work; it was facilitating better decision-making.

"I think this will help tremendously," Marcia said as they wrapped up. "Let's move this to the wall outside our team area where everyone can see it."

"What about our stand-up meetings?" Thomas asked. "Could we hold them at the board instead of in the conference room?"

"That's an excellent idea," Marcia agreed. "Starting tomorrow, let's meet at the board at 9:15 am for a fifteen-minute stand-up to sync on progress and plans."

As they transferred the board to its permanent home, Marcia felt a sense of accomplishment. They'd created something simple yet powerful - a visual representation of their collective work that made invisible problems visible.

Positioned at her desk once more, she emailed Elizabeth with an update:

We've implemented a visual task tracking system to prevent future miscommunications. The authentication module will be delivered to QA by 5 pm today. I'd be happy to show you our new process during your next visit.

Glancing toward the newly installed board, Marcia could already see team members gathered around it, discussing task priorities and dependencies. The colourful cards and clear structure seemed to invite engagement in a way their previous digital tools never had.

The missed deadline had revealed a critical gap in their workflow, but addressing it had created an unexpected opportunity - a system that not only tracked work but transformed how they organised and communicated about it. The task board was more than just a tool; it was becoming a focal point for team collaboration and decision-making.

Now they needed to establish a regular rhythm of using and updating it - a daily practice that would make work visibility a habit rather than an afterthought.

✧   ✧   ✧

"Let's gather around the board, everyone."

Marcia arrived early Thursday morning to find Victor already adjusting the task cards, ensuring they were perfectly aligned on the magnetic whiteboard. He glanced up as she approached.

"I've made a few organisational improvements," he explained, stepping back to reveal a grid system he'd created with thin tape. "Now each swimlane corresponds to a team member, while maintaining our workflow columns."

"That's actually brilliant," Marcia said, impressed by his initiative. "It shows both who's responsible and where work stands."

By 9:15 am, the entire team had assembled around the board. Some carried coffee cups, others scrolled through phones, but all eyes eventually settled on the colourful array of task cards.

"Welcome to our first official daily stand-up," Marcia began. "The format is simple - each person takes about a minute to share three things: what you completed yesterday, what you're working on today, and any obstacles in your way."

Dmitri checked his watch. "Only fifteen minutes for everyone?"

"That's the point," Marcia explained. "It forces us to be concise. This isn't for detailed problem-solving - it's to make work visible and identify issues that need attention later."

She turned to Thomas. "Would you like to start?"

Thomas straightened, clearing his throat. "Yesterday, I completed the automated test framework for the inventory module," he said, moving a blue card from "In Progress" to "Done." "Today, I'll begin implementing similar tests for the reporting features." He moved a yellow card from "To Do" to "In Progress." "My obstacle is that I need updated specifications from Priya before I can complete the test scenarios."

Priya nodded, making a note. "I'll have those to you by noon."

"Perfect," Marcia said. "That's exactly how this should work. Who's next?"

One by one, team members shared their updates, physically moving cards across the board as they spoke. The visual representation made progress - and sticking points - immediately apparent.

When Victor's turn came, he pointed to the authentication module card now in the "Review" column. "As promised, I delivered this yesterday. Today I'm addressing the database optimisation issues we identified through the skills matrix." He paused. "My obstacle is that I need thirty uninterrupted minutes with Jason to discuss the user preference state management, but our schedules haven't aligned."

Jason immediately pulled out his phone. "I'm free at 11:00 am."

"Noted," Victor replied with a nod.

As the stand-up continued, Marcia observed something remarkable happening. Team members weren't just reporting to her - they were committing to each other. When Mei mentioned struggling with a charting component, Dmitri immediately offered help based on his recent experience. When Jason flagged a potential delay with the UI framework, Thomas suggested a workaround he'd used previously.

The physical act of moving cards across the board created a shared sense of progress and accountability that hadn't existed before. Problems weren't hidden in email threads or private task lists - they were visible to everyone, inviting collaborative solutions.

"That's everyone," Marcia said, checking her watch. "Fourteen minutes - not bad for our first attempt."

"What about you?" Mei asked. "Shouldn't you share your updates too?"

Marcia hadn't expected this question but appreciated the inclusion. "You're right, I should. Yesterday I responded to Elizabeth about our authentication module delivery and implemented this board. Today I'll be finalising our resource allocation plan based on the skills matrix. My obstacle is gathering accurate time estimates for the remaining components."

"I can help with that," Victor offered unexpectedly. "I've been tracking actual versus estimated time for my tasks. The data might be useful for calibrating future estimates."

"That would be extremely helpful," Marcia replied, genuinely surprised and pleased by his offer.

As the team dispersed back to their desks, Marcia remained at the board, taking a photo to document their current status. James passed by, pausing to observe.

"How was the first stand-up?" he asked.

"It turned out better than I thought," Marcia offered honestly. "They're already using it to self-organise and solve problems without my intervention."

James nodded approvingly. "That's the real benefit of visual management - it creates a shared reality that drives collective action." He studied the board. "I see Victor added swimlanes."

"His idea entirely," Marcia said. "He came in early to set it up."

"Interesting," James remarked. "The most resistant team members often become the strongest advocates once they see the value." He checked his watch. "Looking forward to seeing how this evolves."

Throughout the day, Marcia noticed team members returning to the board, sometimes alone to move their cards forward, other times in pairs or small groups to discuss dependencies or brainstorm solutions. The board had become more than just a tracking tool - it was becoming a collaboration hub.

By late afternoon, she spotted Thomas and Priya standing together at the board, engaged in animated conversation about test scenarios. Nearby, Victor was explaining something to Jason, pointing at connections between their respective tasks. The physical visualisation had created new opportunities for interaction that their previous siloed approach had prevented.

While Marcia was thinking ahead to the next day's stand-up, she realised they needed to address one more critical aspect of workflow visibility - how to handle tasks that couldn't move forward due to external factors or dependencies. Several cards had been stuck in the "In Progress" column for days, creating the illusion of ongoing work when they were actually blocked.

She drafted a quick proposal for a "Blocked" column with specific requirements for cards placed there - what was blocking the task, who could unblock it, and what actions were being taken. This would make impediments just as visible as progress, encouraging focused effort on removing obstacles rather than starting new work.

Tomorrow's stand-up would be the perfect opportunity to introduce this refinement. With each small improvement to their process, the team was building not just better project tracking but a stronger collaborative culture - one where problems weren't hidden or ignored but acknowledged and addressed together.

❖ ❖ ❖

By Friday, the visual task board had already transformed the team's dynamic. Marcia arrived to find several team members clustered around it, engaged in a focused discussion about dependencies between components.

"Morning," she greeted them. "Looks like you're getting a head start on the stand-up."

Mei smiled. "Thomas found a potential issue with how the reporting module interfaces with the authentication system. We're mapping out the connection points."

Thomas pointed to several cards with green dependency arrows between them. "If we address these in the wrong sequence, we'll create rework. I've been thinking about a better approach."

What struck Marcia most was how this conversation was happening spontaneously, without her initiation. The board had created a natural gathering point where cross-component discussions could happen organically.

As 9:15 am approached, the entire team assembled. Marcia noted that everyone arrived on time - a small but meaningful shift from their previous meeting habits.

"Before we begin," she said, "I'd like to introduce one refinement to our board." She placed a new column header between "In Progress" and "Review" labelled "Blocked" with a red background.

"I've noticed several tasks that can't move forward but are sitting in 'In Progress,' making it look like active work is happening when it's actually stalled."

Victor nodded. "That creates misleading impressions of our productivity."

"Exactly," Marcia continued. "When you place a card in this column, you'll need to add three pieces of information:

what's blocking it, who can help unblock it, and what actions you're taking to resolve the blockage."

She demonstrated with a sample card, writing these details on the back. "This makes impediments visible so we can focus on removing them rather than starting new work while old tasks remain blocked."

The team quickly embraced the concept. During the stand-up, three cards moved into the new Blocked column, each with clear documentation of what was preventing progress.

"The user preference module is blocked because we're waiting on a decision from Elizabeth about data retention policies," Jason explained, placing his card in the red column. "I've drafted three options and sent them to her yesterday. I'll follow up this afternoon if I don't hear back."

This level of transparency was new. Previously, such delays would have been mentioned casually or hidden entirely, creating the impression that work was proceeding when it wasn't.

As the stand-up continued, Marcia observed how each person's update triggered immediate responses from others. When Dmitri mentioned completing the data transformation component, Priya immediately asked if she could review it before end of day. When Victor reported being ahead of schedule on database optimisation, Thomas quickly suggested they meet to implement performance testing.

The board wasn't just tracking work - it was facilitating a web of conversations that might never have happened otherwise.

"Excellent updates," Marcia said as they wrapped up. "Now, something else I'd like to try. Let's take two minutes to look at the board as a whole. What patterns do you notice?"

The team stepped back, studying the visual landscape of their project.

"Most of our blocked items involve waiting for external decisions," Mei observed.

"We have more tasks in progress than we have team members," Victor added. "That seems inefficient."

"The reporting and inventory modules have the most dependencies," Thomas noted, pointing to the cluster of green arrows. "They're becoming bottlenecks."

These insights - immediately obvious on the board but nearly invisible in their previous tracking systems - sparked a brief but productive discussion about how to organise their efforts more effectively.

"Let's try to address these patterns today," Marcia suggested. "Limit work in progress, focus on unblocking critical paths, and communicate clearly about external dependencies."

As the team went their separate way, Sarah Williams from the business analysis team approached Marcia. She approached more quietly this time. "Caught your stand-up - honestly, it was impressive," she admitted, voice lower and less combative. "Mind if I borrow this approach for my team? Our stakeholders are constantly asking for status updates that take hours to compile."

"Of course," Marcia replied. "The physical visibility makes a huge difference in both awareness and accountability."

Sarah studied the board. "I can see exactly where the project stands in thirty seconds. That's powerful." She took a photo with her phone. "Elizabeth will appreciate this level of transparency too."

Throughout the day, Marcia noticed something remarkable - team members were completing tasks and immediately moving their cards rather than waiting for the next stand-up. The board had become a living document that reflected real-time progress.

By late afternoon, two of the three blocked items had moved forward. Jason had received Elizabeth's decision on data retention, and Victor had resolved a technical impediment that had been blocking Mei's work. The visual representation of blockages had created an almost magnetic pull to resolve them.

As Marcia updated her weekly status report for James, she included a photo of the board and a brief summary of the improvements they'd seen: increased collaboration, faster identification and resolution of impediments, and more balanced workload distribution. The metrics were already showing improvement - cycle time for components had decreased by nearly 20% in just three days.

What impressed her most, however, wasn't the efficiency gains but the cultural shift. Team members were taking collective ownership of the project rather than focusing solely on their individual assignments. When Victor finished his tasks early, he immediately helped Dmitri with a challenging database issue. When Priya identified a potential risk in the UI framework, Jason and Mei joined her in a spontaneous brainstorming session at the board.

As she prepared to leave for the weekend, Marcia spotted Thomas adding one final card to the "Done" column with a satisfied smile. Next week would bring new challenges, but now they had a system that made those challenges visible and manageable. More importantly, they had a team that was beginning to function as a cohesive unit rather than a collection of individual contributors.

Now they needed to extend this visibility beyond daily tasks to encompass their longer-term roadmap. Understanding what they were doing today was important, but seeing how it connected to their broader journey would take their collaboration to the next level.

✧ ✧ ✧

Monday morning brought unexpected news - Elizabeth Parker would be visiting the office that afternoon to review the FreshWorks project status in person. Under normal circumstances, this would have triggered a panicked scramble to prepare presentations and compile status reports. But as Marcia announced this during their stand-up meeting, she noticed something different in the team's reaction.

"Perfect timing," Victor said, surprising everyone. "The visual board will show her exactly where we stand."

"Should we create additional views or reports?" Dmitri asked, his old instincts still present.

Marcia shook her head. "Let's show her the real system we're actually using, not something we created just for the meeting."

The stand-up proceeded with its now-familiar rhythm, each team member moving their cards across the board while explaining their focus for the day. What struck Marcia was how comfortable everyone had become with acknowledging challenges openly.

"I'm blocked on the reporting module integration," Mei said matter-of-factly, moving her card to the red column. "The API documentation is inconsistent with the actual implementation. I need thirty minutes with Victor to resolve this."

"Let's meet at 10:30 am," Victor replied without hesitation. "I think I know what's happening there."

This simple exchange would have been unimaginable a week ago, when admitting obstacles felt like confessing failure and asking for help seemed like imposing on others. Now it was just part of their daily workflow.

After the stand-up, Marcia watched the team disperse with purpose. Their daily gathering had evolved from an awkward status meeting into a coordinated alignment session that set the tone for effective collaboration throughout the day.

"The stand-ups are going well," James commented, joining her at the board. "Elizabeth's visit will be a good test of how this system holds up under executive scrutiny."

"Any advice?" Marcia asked.

"Just let the board speak for itself," James suggested. "The transparency it provides is its own best advocate."

By midday, something remarkable happened. Mei moved her previously blocked card from the red column into "Review," then sought out Thomas to begin testing. The thirty-minute conversation with Victor had resolved what might have been days of delay under their old system.

"That was fast," Marcia commented as Mei passed her desk.

"The solution was straightforward once Victor explained the API versioning issue," Mei replied. "In the past, I might have spent hours trying different approaches before finally asking for help. Having the blocked card visible to everyone made it natural to address it immediately."

At 2 pm, Elizabeth Parker arrived, her expression neutral as Marcia led her to the team area.

"I understand you've implemented some new processes," Elizabeth said. "Robert Miller mentioned your team's transformation has been impressive."

"We're making progress," Marcia acknowledged modestly. "The team deserves the credit for embracing these changes so quickly."

As they approached the visual board, several team members were already gathered there, engaged in what appeared to be an impromptu discussion about dependencies between components.

"This is our task tracking system," Marcia explained, gesturing to the board.

Elizabeth studied it silently, taking in the coloured cards, swimlanes, and workflow columns. Her gaze lingered on the blocked column, which currently held only one card.

"Walk me through how this works," she requested.

Rather than answering herself, Marcia turned to the team. "Would someone like to explain our process?"

To her surprise, Dmitri stepped forward. Once the most reticent team member, he now spoke with quiet confidence about their daily stand-ups, how they managed blocked items, and the way the visual system had improved their coordination.

"Before, I might work for days on something only to discover someone else needed it weeks ago or had already solved a similar problem," he explained. "Now we catch those issues immediately."

Marcia winced inside at the extreme transparency, though at least it was honest.

Elizabeth nodded, then asked pointed questions about specific components. The team answered collectively, each person jumping in when the question touched their area of expertise. There was no defensiveness, no finger-pointing - just clear, factual information about status, challenges, and next steps.

"Show me the authentication module," Elizabeth requested. "That was our critical path item."

Victor moved to the board, pointing out the card now in the "Done" column. "We completed it last Wednesday, a day after the original deadline but within the buffer we identified in our revised schedule."

"What about the quality issues Thomas found last week?" Elizabeth asked, referencing a problem that had been flagged in their status call.

"All resolved," Thomas confirmed, pointing to several green check marks he'd added to cards in the "Done" column. "Assuming the developers aren't hiding any last-minute surprises, we should be good." He said with a wry smile. "Oh, and our automated testing framework caught two additional edge cases that we've also addressed."

As the conversation continued, Marcia observed Elizabeth's expression gradually shifting from sceptical to impressed. The board provided an unfiltered view of project reality that no slide deck could match.

"This is remarkably clear," Elizabeth finally said. "I can see exactly where things stand, what's coming next, and where the potential issues are." She gestured to the lone card in the "Blocked" column. "Including what's currently preventing progress."

"That's exactly why we implemented it," Marcia explained. "We needed a single source of truth that everyone could see and update."

Elizabeth took out her phone and snapped several photos of the board. "I'd like to share this approach with our implementation team at FreshWorks. They face similar coordination challenges."

After Elizabeth departed, the team gathered briefly at the board.

"That went well," Jason said, a note of surprise in his voice.

"It went well because we showed her reality, not a polished presentation," Marcia replied. "The visual system speaks for itself."

"What's next?" Mei asked. "This is working for our day-to-day tasks, but I'm still not sure how everything fits into the bigger picture."

It was the perfect opening for Marcia's next planned tool. "That's exactly what we need to address. The task board shows us what we're doing now, but we need a roadmap to show where we're going over the next several months."

She saw interest spark in their eyes. The success of the task board had created momentum and openness to further improvements.

"Let's schedule a roadmap planning session," Marcia suggested. "We can map out our key milestones and dependencies for the remainder of the FreshWorks project and beyond."

As the team returned to their work, Marcia took a moment to update her leadership notebook. The visual management system had built trust both within the team and with their key stakeholder. Now they needed to extend that visibility to their longer-term journey.

✧　✧　✧

Later that afternoon, as the team's energy remained high from Elizabeth's visit, Marcia gathered everyone for a quick huddle.

"Before we wrap for the day, there's something we need to address," she said, moving to a clean whiteboard. "We don't have time now to create a long-term roadmap, but we need better visibility beyond just the current work."

She went on. "Let's create something simpler - a six-week rolling forecast." Marcia drew a grid on the board with weeks across the top and key workstreams down the side. "This isn't detailed planning, just major milestones and dependencies we can see coming."

"Like knowing there's a bridge out ahead on your route," Jason offered.

"Exactly." Marcia handed out markers. "Each of you add your major deliverables for the next six weeks. Don't overthink it - just what you know is coming."

For the next ten minutes, the board filled with color-coded items. Authentication system completion, reporting module integration, testing framework expansion, and many others all being mapped out to weeks.

Marcia noticed how naturally the team was beginning to think beyond their individual tasks. The six-week view wasn't sophisticated, but it was already changing their perspective from reactive to anticipatory.

"We'll update this every three-weeks," Marcia decided. "Drop the three that just passed, add three at the end. Rolling visibility."

"Simple but effective," Thomas approved.

As they photographed the whiteboard for reference, Marcia made a note in her leadership journal:

Six-week rolling forecast implemented. Bridge between daily execution and future roadmap. Team naturally identifying conflicts and dependencies.

Chapter 7
People Management

"Do you have a minute?"

Marcia stood at the entrance to Victor's cubicle, careful not to disrupt the carefully arranged workspace. The visual task board had been a success, and now she wanted to implement the next tool in her leadership toolkit: regular one-on-one meetings with each team member.

Victor glanced up from his monitors, removing one side of his headphones. "Is there a problem with the authentication module?" His immediate assumption of an issue rather than a casual check-in spoke volumes.

"No problems at all," Marcia assured him. "Actually, I'd like to set up regular one-on-one meetings with everyone on the team. Would you have time this afternoon to kick that off?"

Victor's expression shifted from concern to mild confusion. "One-on-one meetings? About what specifically?"

"About whatever you think would be valuable to discuss," Marcia explained. "Your work, your goals, challenges you're facing - the agenda is largely yours."

Victor considered this with characteristic thoroughness. He rubbed his eyes briefly - a gesture that made him look older than his years. The technology landscape had shifted so dramatically over his decades in the field. Sometimes he felt like he was translating between two different languages - the methodical approaches he'd mastered and the agile, collaborative methods younger developers seemed to breathe naturally. "Three o'clock would be acceptable. Thirty minutes?"

"Perfect. We can use the small conference room."

At precisely three o'clock, Victor arrived at the conference room with his laptop and a notepad. Marcia had deliberately arrived early to arrange the space - setting the chairs at right angles rather than across from each other, bringing coffee, and ensuring the lighting was adjusted to reduce the harsh fluorescents that she'd noticed bothered Victor.

"I see you've prepared," Victor commented, noting the arrangement.

"I want these meetings to be comfortable and productive," Marcia replied. "Would you like some coffee?"

As Victor settled in with his coffee (black, no sugar - Marcia had noticed his preference), she opened her notebook to a clean page.

"I have a simple structure I'd like to use for our one-on-ones," she began. "Just a few questions to guide our conversation, but we can go wherever is most useful for you."

Victor nodded, his posture still slightly rigid but attentive.

"First, how are you doing - and I mean genuinely, not just professionally?"

The question seemed to catch Victor off guard. He paused, considering his response carefully.

"I am... functioning adequately," he said finally. "The new visual system has reduced some frustrations regarding task clarity and priority conflicts."

Marcia noted how he framed his well-being in terms of system effectiveness. "And outside of work? Are you taking time to recharge?"

Victor shifted slightly. "I've been working on a personal programming project on weekends - an algorithm for optimising my chess strategy. It's intellectually stimulating."

"That sounds interesting," Marcia said genuinely. "Do you play chess competitively?"

"Semi-competitively. I participate in an online league." A small hint of enthusiasm crept into his typically measured tone.

Marcia made a note - Victor's passion for structured systems extended beyond work, and he valued intellectual challenges. This might offer insights into how to better engage and motivate him.

"Next question," she continued. "Do you have enough to work on, or too much?"

Victor seemed on firmer ground with this topic. "The current allocation is appropriate. The skills matrix has improved task distribution significantly. I'm no longer addressing basic database queries that others could handle, which allows me to focus on architectural concerns."

"That's good to hear. And is there anything you need from me to be more effective?"

This question prompted a longer pause. Victor seemed to be internally debating something.

"There is one matter," he finally said. "The open office environment presents challenges for focused work, particularly when complex problem-solving is required. The noise, movement, and unpredictable interruptions make sustained concentration difficult."

Marcia nodded, understanding immediately. "What would help with that?"

"Designated quiet hours might be beneficial," Victor suggested. "Perhaps a protocol where non-urgent questions are collected for specific times rather than raised immediately."

"That's a thoughtful solution," Marcia said, writing it down. "It balances your need for focused time with the team's need for collaboration. I'll work on implementing something like that."

Victor's posture relaxed slightly, and for a brief moment, his perpetual watchfulness softened. An uncharacteristic hesitation that revealed something beneath his usual certainty, "That would be... helpful."

"Is there anything else you need?"

After a further moment's consideration, Victor said, "Clarity on technical decision authority would be valuable. Under Carl's leadership, the process was inconsistent - sometimes democratic, sometimes hierarchical, often dependent on who advocated most forcefully rather than technical merit."

This aligned perfectly with what Marcia had observed. "How would you structure the decision process if it were up to you?"

Something shifted in Victor's expression - a subtle but noticeable change. Being asked for his perspective on process design clearly engaged him.

"I would implement a tiered approach," he began, warming to the topic. "Routine decisions could be made by whoever is responsible for the component. Decisions affecting multiple components would require consultation with all affected parties. Architectural decisions with long-term implications would benefit from a more formal review process with explicit criteria."

As he outlined his thoughtful framework, Marcia realised something important - Victor wasn't just a technical expert; he was a systems thinker who could contribute valuable process insights if given the right opportunities.

"Would you be willing to draft that framework more formally?" she asked. "We could review it together and then present it to the team."

Victor straightened, something like surprise flickering across his features. "You want me to design the technical decision process?"

"Who better?" Marcia replied honestly. "You understand the technical considerations and have clearly given this significant thought."

For the first time since she'd known him, Victor smiled - a small but genuine expression. "I would find that valuable. I could have a draft by Friday."

As their meeting continued, Marcia asked about his career aspirations and areas where he wanted to develop. Victor spoke more freely now, revealing a methodical plan for his professional growth and specific technical areas where he sought mastery.

When their thirty minutes concluded, Victor placed his notepad on top of his laptop. "This was unexpectedly productive," he said. "Will these meetings be a regular occurrence?"

"Every two weeks," Marcia confirmed. "Same time?"

"That would be appropriate. I'll calendar it accordingly."

As Victor left, Marcia remained to review her notes. The one-on-one had revealed dimensions to Victor she hadn't fully appreciated - his structured thinking extended beyond code to processes and systems, his challenges with the work environment weren't personal preferences but genuine barriers to his effectiveness, and he responded positively to being asked for his expertise on matters beyond immediate technical tasks.

Most importantly, she'd discovered a way to engage Victor more deeply in the team's evolution - by inviting him to design systems and processes that leveraged his analytical strengths. This wasn't just about accommodating his work style; it was about creating opportunities for him to contribute in ways that aligned with his unique abilities.

Marcia added one final note: *Test quiet hours protocol. Ask Victor to develop technical decision framework. Consider involving him in other process designs.* The one-on-one had accomplished exactly what she'd hoped - it had given her insights she couldn't have gained in group settings or casual interactions.

As she prepared for her next meeting with Mei, Marcia reflected on how different each conversation would likely be. Effective people management wasn't about applying the same approach to everyone; it was about understanding each person's unique needs, motivations, and potential contributions - then creating the conditions for them to thrive.

✧   ✧   ✧

The morning after her one-on-one with Victor, Marcia decided to try another approach from the Team Leaders Toolbox: informal desk visits. While scheduled meetings had their place, she'd learned that some insights only emerged in people's natural work environments.

Coffee in hand, she began a casual walk through the team area. The visual task board had already changed since yesterday - Thomas had moved two cards to the "Done" column, and Jason had started on a new UI component. The board was becoming a living record of their progress, updated in real-time rather than during formal check-ins.

She approached Dmitri's desk first, noticing the dark circles under his eyes had faded since she'd insisted on more sustainable work hours.

"Morning, Dmitri. How's the reporting module coming along?"

He looked up, minimising his code editor. "Good morning. It's progressing well. The frameworks Thomas implemented have caught several edge cases I would have missed."

"That's great to hear," Marcia said, remaining standing to keep the conversation casual. "Do you have what you need to be successful with it?"

Dmitri seemed to consider this question carefully - something Marcia had noticed he often did, weighing his words before speaking.

"Actually, I've been meaning to ask about development environments," he said finally. "Currently, we each maintain our own local setup, which means inconsistent configurations. This creates problems when code works on one machine but fails on another."

"That sounds frustrating," Marcia said. "What would solve that issue?"

"A standardised development environment," Dmitri explained, warming to the topic. "We might be able to achieve that using Linux Containers, but honestly, a template Virtual Machine is the safer bet. It would ensure everyone has identical configurations."

"That makes a lot of sense," Marcia said, making a note. "Would you be willing to research some options and make a recommendation?"

Something shifted in Dmitri's expression - a hint of surprise followed by a subtle straightening, not just of his posture but in purpose. "I would be happy to. I have experience with VMware from a previous project."

"Perfect. Maybe you could prepare a short proposal by next week? Nothing formal - just options and trade-offs."

Dmitri nodded, and Marcia noticed a new energy in his demeanour. It was a subtle shift - from someone who endured work to someone who shaped it. Like Victor yesterday, he seemed to respond positively to being asked for his expertise beyond his assigned tasks.

Moving on, she stopped by Mei's workspace, which was characteristically personalised with small plants and family photos.

"Those charts are looking good," Marcia commented, gesturing to Mei's screen where colourful data visualisations were taking shape.

"Thanks! Jason helped with the interaction design," Mei said. "It's so much easier now that we're collaborating based on skills rather than strict component ownership."

"I'm glad that's working well," Marcia said. "How are you feeling about your workload? I noticed you took on the user documentation in addition to your development tasks."

Mei hesitated slightly. "I don't mind the documentation - I'm good at it. But sometimes I worry I get pigeonholed into communication tasks because I'm seen as the 'people person.'"

This confirmed something Marcia had observed - Mei's interpersonal skills sometimes overshadowed recognition of her technical capabilities.

"That's a fair concern," Marcia acknowledged. "Would you prefer to focus more exclusively on technical work?"

"Not necessarily," Mei replied thoughtfully. "I actually enjoy the variety. But I'd like equal recognition for both contributions. The skills matrix helped with that - seeing my technical strengths documented alongside my communication skills."

"I understand," Marcia said. "What would make you feel more balanced in that regard?"

Mei thought for a moment. "Maybe opportunities to lead technical discussions or design sessions? I have ideas about the UI architecture that I haven't had a chance to share."

"That's a great suggestion," Marcia said. "The team meeting on Friday will include planning for the next phase - would you be willing to facilitate the UI architecture portion?"

Mei's face brightened. "I'd love to!"

As their conversation concluded, Marcia made another mental note: Mei needed opportunities to demonstrate technical leadership, not just interpersonal skills.

At Thomas's desk, she found him surrounded by testing documentation, methodically working through scenarios.

"How's the automated testing framework going?" she asked.

"Extremely well," Thomas replied, his usual reserve giving way to subtle enthusiasm. "Automated defect detection has improved by 23% since implementation."

"That's impressive," Marcia said. "Is there anything you need to expand its effectiveness?"

Thomas adjusted his glasses. "Access to a dedicated test environment would help. Currently, I'm working around development environment constraints, which limits some testing scenarios."

"Let me look into that," Marcia promised. "Dmitri is actually researching environment standardisation options - perhaps you two could coordinate?"

"That makes sense," Thomas agreed. "A comprehensive approach would benefit both development and testing."

As she moved on to Jason's desk, Marcia was struck by how these brief, informal conversations were revealing practical needs she might never have learned about in scheduled meetings. The physical presence at each person's workspace created a different dynamic - more casual, more immediate, and often more honest.

Jason was sketching UI wireframes when she approached, his desk cluttered with paper prototypes.

"These look interesting," Marcia commented, gesturing to the sketches.

"I'm trying a new approach to the mobile experience," Jason explained. "Our current design doesn't scale well to smaller screens."

"I didn't realise mobile optimisation was a priority," Marcia said.

"It wasn't officially," Jason admitted. "But I noticed in the requirements that 30% of users will access the system via tablets. Our current approach would create a poor experience for them."

This was valuable information - Jason had identified a potential issue by reading between the lines of requirements, something that might have been missed in their formal planning.

"That's good initiative," Marcia said. "What would help you move this forward?"

"Some time with Priya to align on the business requirements for mobile users," Jason replied. "And maybe access to the UI design tools we used on previous projects - I don't have licenses for them."

"I'll follow up on both fronts," Marcia promised.

By the time she completed her rounds, Marcia had filled two pages in her notebook with specific needs, suggestions, and observations. The desk visits had revealed tangible issues she could address immediately - environment standardisation, test infrastructure, design tools - as well as opportunities to better leverage individual strengths.

Settling in comfortably at her desk, she organised her notes into actionable items, prioritising them based on impact and effort. Some, like connecting Thomas and Dmitri to collaborate on environment standardisation, required nothing more than a quick email. Others, like securing design tool licenses for Jason, would need budget approval.

What struck her most was how different these conversations had been from the formal one-on-one with Victor. The casual setting had elicited practical, immediate concerns rather than broader career or process discussions.

Both approaches had their place in understanding the team's needs.

James passed by her desk, noticing her detailed notes. "Desk visits?" he asked with a knowing smile.

"Yes," Marcia confirmed. "Amazing what you learn just by showing up where people work."

"The best leaders are visible and accessible," James agreed. "Find anything surprising?"

"Several things," Marcia replied. "Technical needs I wasn't aware of, collaboration opportunities, and some insights into how people want to grow. It's given me a much clearer picture of what the team actually needs versus what I thought they needed."

As James continued on his way, Marcia turned back to her notes. The team goals had aligned their purpose, the skills matrix had mapped their capabilities, and the visual board had made their work visible. Now these personal connections were helping her understand the human element - what each person needed to thrive and contribute their best.

The team was becoming more than the sum of its parts.

✧ ✧ ✧

Marcia sat alone in the conference room during lunch, a blank document open on her laptop titled "Leadership Approach." The morning's desk visits had revealed so many individual needs and perspectives that she felt the need to organise her thoughts about how she wanted to lead this team.

James had mentioned something called a "Line Management Manifesto" in the Team Leaders Toolbox - a personal document outlining leadership principles and commitments. Unlike team goals that were shared publicly, this was meant to be a private north star to guide her decisions and actions.

She began typing:

My Leadership Commitments:
1. I will listen before acting, seeking to understand each team member's unique perspective, strengths, and challenges.

Thinking of Victor's need for quiet focus time and Mei's desire for technical recognition, she continued:

2. I will recognise that each person has different needs and motivators - what works for one may not work for another.

The morning's desk visits had revealed practical needs she wouldn't have discovered otherwise:

3. I will be present and visible, not just in meetings but in day-to-day work environments.

She paused, reflecting on what she'd learned about her team over the past week. The skills matrix had revealed hidden capabilities, while one-on-ones and desk visits had surfaced personal goals and frustrations.

4. I will create opportunities for growth that align with individual aspirations, not just project needs.

"Mind if I join you?"

James stood at the door, sandwich in hand. Marcia instinctively moved to minimise her document, then stopped herself.

"Not at all. I'm working on that leadership manifesto you mentioned."

James sat across from her, deliberately angling his chair so he couldn't see her screen. "That's one of my favourite tools -

clarifies your own thinking about leadership before you try to apply it to others."

"I'm finding it surprisingly challenging," Marcia spoke with quiet honesty. "It's making me question assumptions I didn't realise I had."

"Like what?" James asked, unwrapping his sandwich.

"Like the idea that good management looks the same for everyone. After just a week of conversations, I'm seeing how different each team member's needs are. Victor thrives with clear processes and quiet focus time. Mei wants recognition for her technical abilities alongside her interpersonal skills. Thomas needs infrastructure for testing excellence."

James nodded. "The best leaders are chameleons - adapting their approach to each situation and person while maintaining consistent principles."

"That's what I'm trying to capture," Marcia said, gesturing to her screen. "What are my non-negotiable principles, and where will I adapt?"

"And what have you discovered?" James asked, genuinely curious.

Marcia thought for a moment. "That I value transparency, individual growth, and creating systems that help people do their best work. But how those values translate into actions will look different for each person."

"That's a powerful insight," James said. "Many leaders never get there - they keep trying to find the one perfect leadership style, when what works best is thoughtful adaptation."

"The desk visits this morning were eye-opening," Marcia continued. "I learned more in thirty minutes of casual conversations than I might have in hours of formal meetings."

"Different formats reveal different information," James agreed. "That's why the toolkit includes multiple approaches to people management. One-on-ones, desk visits, team meetings - each creates a different kind of conversation."

Marcia returned to her document, adding another principle:

5. I will create different spaces for communication - formal and informal, scheduled and spontaneous, individual and group - recognising that different insights emerge in different contexts.

"I see another challenge coming," James said, finishing his sandwich. "Once you've established these principles, the hard part becomes living them consistently, especially under pressure."

Marcia nodded, thinking about how easily good intentions could be overwhelmed by deadlines and crises. "That's why I'm writing this now, while things are relatively calm. It gives me something to refer back to when decisions get tough."

James stood to leave. "One final thought - the best manifestos also include how you want to be held accountable. What should your team do if you drift from these commitments?"

This struck Marcia as both important and uncomfortable. The idea of explicitly inviting feedback on her leadership felt vulnerable, but also necessary.

After James left, she added a final section:

If I drift from these commitments, I want my team to: - Remind me of these principles directly and respectfully - Help me understand the impact of my actions or decisions - Suggest specific alternatives that would better align with these commitments

She saved the document, printed a copy, and tucked it into her notebook. Unlike the team goals poster hanging prominently on the wall, this personal manifesto would stay private - but its influence would be felt in every interaction, decision, and system she created. In this way, her commitments, and the ability for her team to hold her accountable would be built into the teams culture.

As Marcia returned to her desk, she noticed Thomas and Dmitri engaged in what appeared to be a productive conversation about environment standardisation. Nearby, Mei was showing Jason something on her screen, gesturing animatedly while he nodded with interest.

The team was connecting in new ways, forming collaborations that crossed their previous boundaries. Her leadership approach was already bearing fruit, creating conditions where everyone could contribute their unique strengths to a shared purpose.

Robert Miller passed through the team area, pausing briefly to study the visual task board. He smiled as Marcia caught his eye before continuing on his way. The founder's silent acknowledgment confirmed what Marcia was beginning to feel - they were becoming a true team, not just a collection of talented individuals.

That afternoon, she received an email from Elizabeth Parker:

Hi Marcia,

Our implementation team was impressed by the visual management approach you shared. Could you send more details on your daily stand-up process and how you're managing blocked items? We'd like to implement something similar.

Also, the latest build quality is noticeably improved. Whatever changes you've made to your QA processes are working.

- Elizabeth

The email reinforced what Marcia was learning - good leadership wasn't about heroic individual effort or charismatic inspiration. It was about creating the right conditions, systems, and connections that enabled everyone to do their best work together.

The line management manifesto would be her guide in building those conditions - a personal reminder of the leader she aspired to be, even on the most challenging days.

✧ ✧ ✧

Friday afternoon arrived with a sense of accomplishment hovering over the Enterprise Solutions team. The visual task board showed significant progress - more cards in the "Done" column than any previous week, and only one item remaining in the "Blocked" section. The daily stand-ups had become smoother and more focused, with team members naturally coordinating their efforts without Marcia's intervention.

"Got a minute?" James appeared at Marcia's desk, glancing at the notes she was reviewing.

"For you? Always," she replied, closing her notebook.

"I'd like to hear how your people management approach is developing," he said, pulling up a chair. "One-on-ones, desk visits, leadership principles - how's it all coming together?"

Marcia considered the question. "It's been eye-opening. Each tool reveals different aspects of what the team needs. The one-on-ones give me deeper insights into individual motivations and career goals, while the desk visits uncover practical, day-to-day obstacles I might have missed otherwise."

"And how are you applying those insights?" James asked.

"In more ways than I expected," Marcia acknowledged with a thoughtful smile. "For example, Victor thrives with clear processes and uninterrupted focus time, so we've implemented 'quiet hours' from 1-3 pm where non-urgent questions are held for later. Mei wants more recognition for her technical skills, so she's leading the UI architecture discussion in today's team meeting."

James nodded approvingly. "You're not just collecting information - you're taking action on it."

"The real breakthrough came from connecting people based on what I learned," Marcia continued. "Dmitri mentioned environment standardisation during my desk visit, which aligned perfectly with Thomas's need for better testing infrastructure. Now they're collaborating on a solution that serves both needs."

"That's the multiplier effect of good people management," James said. "You're not just solving individual problems - you're creating connections that generate new solutions."

Marcia glanced toward the team area, where those connections were visibly playing out. Victor and Priya were reviewing database queries together, while Jason showed Mei something on his screen that made her laugh. Even Thomas, typically reserved, was engaged in conversation with Dmitri at the task board.

"The team feels different," Marcia observed. "There's an energy that wasn't there before."

"That's what happens when people feel seen and valued," James replied. "They bring their full selves to work."

As they spoke, Elizabeth Parker arrived for her weekly project review. Instead of heading directly to Marcia's desk as usual, she paused to observe the team interactions.

"Elizabeth," Marcia greeted her, standing to join her. "Early for our meeting?"

"I wanted to see your team in action," Elizabeth replied. "When you're late, I'm the one who has to explain why. I've been burned before, so don't make me defend you unless you are going to deliver." She paused, letting the weight of her words settle. "There's a noticeable difference from just three weeks ago."

"We've implemented several changes," Marcia explained.

"Clearly," Elizabeth said. "The status report shows you've made up ground on the timeline, quality metrics are trending positively, and that visual board," She gestured toward the task board. "Has given us better visibility than months of traditional reporting."

"The team deserves the credit," Marcia said. "They've embraced every new approach we've tried."

Elizabeth's typical business-focused expression softened slightly. "It's more than that. Teams don't transform this quickly without effective leadership." She checked her watch. "Shall we discuss the details in our meeting?"

As Elizabeth headed to the conference room, James gave Marcia some gentle encouragement. "She's right, you know. The tools are just enablers - it's how you've applied them that's making the difference."

The team meeting that afternoon served as a perfect demonstration of how far they'd come. Mei confidently led the UI architecture discussion, with Jason and Priya building on her ideas. Victor presented his framework for technical decision-making - a tiered approach that balanced individual autonomy with collective input on decisions affecting multiple components.

Most striking was how they handled disagreements. When Thomas and Dmitri had different perspectives on the testing approach, they discussed the trade-offs openly, focusing on the merits rather than defending positions. The team's shared goals provided a framework for resolving conflicts that might have previously devolved into personal disagreements.

"Before we wrap up," Marcia said as the meeting neared its end, "I'd like to acknowledge something important. The changes we've implemented over the past three weeks - team goals, skills matrix, visual management, revised communication approaches - have been successful because each of you has contributed to shaping them."

She glanced around the table, making eye contact with each person. "This wasn't about imposing a new system on you, but about creating the conditions where your collective talents could shine. And that's exactly what's happening."

Victor, usually reserved with praise, spoke up. "The systematic approach has been... effective. Clear processes, defined decision frameworks, and appropriate allocation of tasks based on skills - these are logical improvements."

"And it feels different too," Mei added. "There's more trust. We're actually talking to each other instead of just reporting status."

Dmitri nodded. "For the first time since I joined this team, I believe we will deliver what we promised - on time and with quality."

As the group broke apart after the meeting, Marcia remained at the table, reflecting on their journey. The transformation wasn't complete - they still had challenging technical problems to solve and a demanding timeline to meet. But the foundation was now in place: shared goals, visible work, matched skills, and most importantly, individuals who felt valued for their unique contributions.

James had been right about the multiplier effect. By understanding each person's needs and strengths, she'd been able to create connections that generated more value than any individual contribution could have achieved alone. Victor's process design complemented Thomas's quality focus. Mei's communication skills enhanced Jason's technical innovations. Dmitri's system thinking supported Priya's user-centred approach.

The tools from the Team Leaders Toolbox had provided the framework, but the real magic happened when those tools were applied with genuine care for each person's growth and success.

Later that evening, as she prepared to leave for the weekend, Marcia noticed someone had added a new element to their team goals poster - a small graph tracking their key metrics, showing steady improvement over the past few weeks. Next to it was a handwritten note: "What gets measured gets managed. What gets celebrated gets repeated."

She smiled, recognising Mei's handwriting. The team wasn't just following a new process - they were making it their own, adding their unique touches and insights.

Monday would bring new challenges. They still needed to develop a comprehensive roadmap to guide their longer-term journey. Resource allocation needed more formal structure to prevent the return of unsustainable workloads. Communication with stakeholders beyond Elizabeth would require additional attention.

But for now, Marcia allowed herself to appreciate how far they'd come. People management wasn't just about handling personnel issues or conducting performance reviews. It was about creating an environment where each person could contribute their best work while growing in the direction of their aspirations.

As she headed to the elevator, Marcia spotted Robert Miller speaking with James near the executive offices. They both glanced her way, and Robert gave a wave of acknowledgment before returning to their conversation.

For Marcia, a simple wave mean Robert knew who she was, that he knew she was making a difference on the FreshWorks project, and that he trusted her and she had his support.

The Enterprise Solutions team was becoming what Marcia had hoped for - not just a group of talented individuals, but a true team with shared purpose, mutual respect, and collective ownership of their success.

Chapter 8
What's On This Week Email

Monday morning greeted Marcia with a fresh challenge. The team had made remarkable progress with their internal systems - team goals, skills matrix, visual task board, and improved people management. But as she reviewed her calendar for the week, she realised they were missing a critical element: consistent communication with stakeholders beyond Elizabeth Parker.

Several department heads had sent emails over the weekend asking for updates on different aspects of the FreshWorks project. Robert Miller had requested a brief overview for the executive leadership meeting on Wednesday. And Sarah from Business Analysis needed to coordinate requirements for the next development phase.

As team leader, Marcia had been fielding these requests individually, but the approach wasn't sustainable. Each response took time away from her other responsibilities, and the information often became outdated almost as soon as she sent it.

There has to be a better way. She scrolled through yet another request for project status.

She opened the Team Leaders Toolbox folder and turned to the section on communication tools. The first recommendation caught her eye: "What's on This Week

Email." The concept was simple but powerful - a regular, structured update sent to stakeholders and team members that outlined priorities, achievements, and upcoming activities.

As she read through the guidance, Marcia realised this could solve multiple problems at once. It would create a consistent communication rhythm, reduce ad-hoc status requests, and help the team stay aligned on priorities.

After sketching a quick template, Marcia headed to the stand-up meeting, where the team was already gathering around the visual task board.

"Great progress last week," she began after everyone had shared their updates. "But I've noticed we're spending a lot of time responding to stakeholder questions about what we're working on."

Nods around the circle confirmed this was a shared frustration.

"I'd like to implement a weekly update email," Marcia continued. "A simple, consistent message that goes out every Monday morning with our achievements, current focus, and upcoming activities."

"That sounds logical," Victor said. "Structured communication is more efficient than repeated ad-hoc updates."

"Who would write this email?" Dmitri asked, his expression suggesting he was concerned about additional work.

"Initially, I'll draft it," Marcia replied. "But I'll need input from each of you on your areas."

After the stand-up, Marcia returned to her desk and began drafting the first "What's on This Week" email. She kept the format simple:

Subject: FreshWorks Project - What's on This Week (May 13-17)

Hi Team,

Here's our focus for this week and a recap of recent achievements:

Last Week's Achievements:
- *Completed authentication module integration and testing (Victor, Thomas)*
- *Deployed automated testing framework for critical components (Thomas)*
- *Finalised database optimisation for reporting module (Dmitri)*
- *Established environment standardisation requirements (Dmitri, Thomas)*

This Week's Focus:
- *Complete user preference module (Jason)*
- *Finalise chart visualisation components (Mei)*
- *Integrate reporting module with authentication system (Dmitri)*
- *Implement first phase of automated testing across all components (Thomas)*

Upcoming Milestones:
- *May 24: Reporting module delivery*
- *May 31: User acceptance testing begins*
- *June 14: Phase 1 deployment*

Blockers/Needs:
- *Awaiting client decision on data retention policies (expected May 17)*
- *Need final business requirements for international user access*

Please let me know if you have questions or need additional information.
Marcia

She reviewed the draft, satisfied that it captured essential information without overwhelming detail. Before sending it out, she shared it with the team for review.

"This looks comprehensive," Mei commented. "But maybe we could add a brief 'wins' section? Something that celebrates specific successes or milestones reached?"

"Good idea," Marcia agreed, adding the section.

"The emphasis on blockers is helpful," Thomas noted. "It makes our needs visible to those who can address them."

Victor studied the email with his characteristic thoroughness. "The structure is logical and the information density appropriate. I would add version numbers to the components mentioned for precise tracking."

With their feedback incorporated, Marcia sent the email to the team, Elizabeth Parker, Robert Miller, Sarah from Business Analysis, and other key stakeholders. Almost immediately, she received positive responses.

Hi Marcia,
This is exactly what I needed. Now I can better coordinate the business requirements with your development timeline.
Regards,
Sarah

Robert Miller's response was typically brief but affirming:

Excellent format. I have what I need for Wednesday. Continue weekly.

As Marcia turned to her other tasks for the day, she reflected on how such a simple tool could have such immediate impact. The 'What's on This Week' email wasn't just pushing information out - it was creating a rhythm that both the team and stakeholders could rely on, reducing uncertainty and setting clear expectations.

Later that afternoon, James made his usual stop at her desk. "I see you've implemented the weekly update," he said, glancing at her screen. "How's the response been?"

"Overwhelmingly positive," Marcia replied. "I think we've been underestimating how much uncertainty affects everyone. Having a regular, predictable communication pattern seems to create confidence, even when the news isn't all good."

James nodded. "That's the secret most leaders miss. People can handle challenges and even bad news - what they struggle with is unpredictability. A consistent rhythm creates trust, even during difficult times." After a brief pause, James added sincerely, "You are doing great work leading the team. Keep it up."

Marcia didn't say anything, but mentally noted the encouragement.

As James continued on his way, Marcia added a reminder to her calendar to prepare next week's update. This wasn't just a one-time communication - it needed to become a reliable habit that stakeholders could count on.

At the end of the day, she noticed something unexpected. The usual Monday afternoon barrage of status request emails hadn't materialised. The single, comprehensive update had apparently satisfied most stakeholders' immediate information needs, freeing her and the team to focus on actual work instead of constantly reporting on it.

Victor approached her desk as she was preparing to leave. "The update email was effective," he said with characteristic directness. "Three separate managers who normally query me directly about authentication progress referenced your email instead."

Coming from Victor, this was high praise indeed.

The "What's on This Week" email had proven its value on day one, but its real impact would come from consistency - becoming a reliable part of their team's operating rhythm that stakeholders could depend on.

Tomorrow, Marcia would focus on their weekly team meeting format. The stand-ups were working well for daily coordination, but they needed a forum for deeper discussions and collaborative problem-solving. With the communication rhythm beginning to take shape, the next challenge was creating space for the team to align not just on tasks, but on ideas and innovations that would drive their collective success.

✧ ✧ ✧

"Is this really the best use of our time?"

Victor's question hung in the air as the team sat around the conference table on Tuesday afternoon. Marcia had called a special meeting to discuss restructuring their weekly team gatherings, but fifteen minutes in, they were already hitting resistance.

"I understand your concern," Marcia replied. "But our current weekly meetings aren't working. They've become status updates that duplicate our daily stand-ups, with little time for actual problem-solving or collaboration."

She motioned toward the whiteboard where she'd sketched a proposed new format:

1. Brief updates (5 minutes)
2. Theme of the week (20 minutes)
3. Collaborative problem-solving (20 minutes)
4. Open forum (15 minutes)

"The 'What's on This Week' email is handling status communication," Marcia continued. "That frees our face-to-face time for things that actually benefit from being in the same room together."

Mei nodded enthusiastically. "I like the idea of a weekly theme. It could help us tackle bigger issues that get lost in day-to-day tasks."

"And the open forum would give everyone a voice," Jason added. "Sometimes I have ideas or questions that don't fit anywhere else."

Dmitri looked sceptical. "What exactly would these 'themes' involve? I'm concerned about adding theoretical discussions when we have practical work to complete."

It was a fair question. Marcia needed to make this concrete for the team to see its value.

"Let me give you an example," she said, walking to the whiteboard. "Last week, several of you mentioned challenges with our code review process. It's inconsistent, feedback comes too late, and sometimes critical issues are missed."

She wrote "CODE REVIEW PROCESS" on the board.

"That could be next week's theme. We'd spend twenty minutes discussing the current process, identifying pain points, and brainstorming improvements. By the end, we'd have actionable next steps for making it better."

Thomas adjusted his glasses twice - a nervous habit. Something about the team's energy today felt different, safer somehow. For once, he didn't wait to be directly asked for his opinion, "That would actually be valuable. Our current approach is inefficient and lacks clear standards."

Victor's expression had shifted from sceptical to thoughtful. "If the themes address actual workflow obstacles, that could be productive."

"Exactly," Marcia said. "These aren't abstract discussions - they're focused on removing real barriers to our effectiveness."

She moved to a clear whiteboard area. "Let's try something. What are the top three issues slowing us down or causing frustration right now? Things that don't get addressed in our daily stand-ups?"

The team began calling out challenges: inconsistent development environments, unclear prioritisation when requirements change, difficulties coordinating with the business team, technical debt that never gets addressed.

As Marcia captured these on the whiteboard, energy in the room noticeably shifted. These were issues everyone faced but rarely had a forum to discuss systematically.

"These would all make excellent weekly themes," she said. "And the beauty is that we'd actually make decisions and take action, not just talk about problems."

"What about the collaborative problem-solving section?" Dmitri asked. "How would that differ from the theme discussion?"

"The theme would be planned in advance - a topic we know needs attention," Marcia explained. "The problem-solving section would address whatever urgent issue has emerged that week. Something that needs multiple perspectives to resolve."

She could see the concept was starting to resonate, but there was still hesitation.

"Let's try it for four weeks," she suggested. "If it's not adding value, we'll adjust or go back to our current format."

The team agreed to the trial period, and Marcia moved on to implementation details.

"I'd like to hold these meetings on Wednesday afternoons," she said. "That gives us time to compile discussion topics from Monday and Tuesday, while still leaving enough week to act on any decisions we make."

"Who will facilitate the meetings?" Mei asked.

"Initially, I will," Marcia replied. "But eventually, I'd like to rotate that responsibility, especially for the theme discussions.

If you're particularly knowledgeable or passionate about a topic, you might lead that portion."

Victor looked alarmed at this prospect, but Marcia quickly added, "Only if you're comfortable, of course. The goal isn't to put people on the spot but to leverage everyone's strengths."

As they worked through the logistics, Marcia felt the initial resistance giving way to cautious optimism. By the meeting's end, they had agreed on the new format, a rotation schedule for the first four themes, and criteria for evaluating success.

Once she returned to her workspace, Marcia updated the team calendar with the new meeting structure and sent a quick follow-up email outlining the changes. She added a section to her "What's on This Week" template to highlight the upcoming theme, giving everyone time to prepare.

James dropped in again as she was finishing. "How did the meeting format discussion go?"

"Rocky start, but we got there," Marcia replied. "Everyone eventually saw the value once we focused on concrete issues that frustrate them daily."

James nodded knowingly. "The key to any process change is showing people how it solves their actual problems, not just creating theoretical improvements."

"Exactly," Marcia agreed. "I think everyone left feeling cautiously optimistic."

"And how does this fit with your other communication tools?"

"It completes the picture," Marcia explained. "The daily stand-ups handle tactical coordination, the 'What's on This Week' email manages stakeholder communication, and now the weekly team meeting provides space for deeper collaboration and problem-solving."

James smiled approvingly. "You're building a complete communication ecosystem. Each piece serves a different purpose but works together as a whole." After a brief pause, James added, "You are doing great work Marcia, thank you."

As he left, Marcia reflected on his observation. It wasn't enough to have individual communication tools - they needed to form a cohesive system that addressed different needs without duplication or gaps. And beneath that thought, a small sense of warmth settled in her chest. James had noticed. He'd seen her effort, named it, and thanked her. For a moment, she let herself appreciate that - not just the compliment, but the recognition from someone whose opinion she genuinely valued.

Maybe, just maybe, she could be a team leader after all.

The next day, she posted the first four weekly themes on the wall near their visual task board:

Week 1: Code Review Process
Week 2: Development Environment Standardisation
Week 3: Requirement Change Management
Week 4: Technical Debt Strategy

Throughout the day, she noticed team members stopping to look at the list. Dmitri and Thomas were discussing the environment standardisation topic near the coffee machine. Later, she overheard Victor explaining to Jason how he had improved code review processes at his previous company.

The simple act of naming these issues and creating designated time to address them had already sparked conversations that wouldn't have happened otherwise.

By Friday, anticipation for the new meeting format had grown. Team members had started jotting notes about the code review process on a dedicated section of their whiteboard. Even Victor, initially the most resistant, had contributed several detailed observations.

As Marcia made preparations for the weekend, she reflected on the week's progress. Their communication system was taking shape.

Each element served a distinct purpose while reinforcing the others. Together, they created a rhythm that brought predictability and focus to work that had previously felt chaotic and reactive.

Next week would be the first test of their new meeting format. If successful, it would add the final piece to their communication ecosystem - a regular forum for addressing the larger systemic issues that determined their long-term effectiveness, not just their day-to-day progress.

The pieces were falling into place, one systematic improvement at a time.

✧ ✧ ✧

"Alright, who wants to start our code review discussion?"

Wednesday afternoon had arrived, and with it, the first test of their newly structured team meeting. The conference room felt different somehow - Marcia had arranged the chairs in a circle rather than around the table, and a large whiteboard displayed their agenda with the theme "Code Review Process" prominently featured.

The team exchanged glances, no one immediately volunteering. Even Mei, usually quick to jump in, seemed to be waiting.

"I can begin," Victor said, surprising everyone. He stood and moved to the whiteboard. "I've documented our current approach and identified three key weaknesses."

As Victor diagrammed their existing process with remarkable clarity, Marcia noticed how the team leaned forward, engaged in a way they rarely had been during previous meetings. Victor framed the problems as process issues rather than individual failures.

"Our first weakness is timing," he explained, circling a section of his diagram. "Reviews happen too late in development, when changes are costly and disruptive."

"That's because we only submit code when we think it's finished," Jason added. "But by then, we're already invested in our approach."

Thomas nodded. "And reviewers feel pressure to approve rather than request significant changes."

The conversation flowed naturally, with each person building on others' observations rather than defending territory. Dmitri highlighted inconsistent standards across different components. Mei noted how knowledge wasn't being effectively shared through the process. Priya explained the challenges from a business requirements perspective.

Marcia facilitated lightly, occasionally asking clarifying questions or redirecting when the discussion drifted, but mostly letting the team's collective intelligence drive the conversation. This was exactly what she'd hoped for. Collaborative problem-solving that leveraged everyone's insights.

Thirty minutes in - ten minutes longer than planned, but Marcia chose not to interrupt the productive flow - they had identified five specific improvements:

1. Earlier "design review" before code is written
2. Smaller, more frequent reviews rather than large batches
3. Documented standards for each component
4. Rotation of reviewers to spread knowledge
5. Automated checks for common issues

"This is excellent," Marcia said as Victor finished noting the last item. "Now comes the crucial part - who will take responsibility for implementing each of these improvements?"

She half-expected hesitation, but hands went up immediately. Victor volunteered to document standards. Thomas offered to research automated checking tools. Mei suggested she could create a rotation schedule and templates for design reviews.

"I'm impressed," Marcia said honestly. "You've not only identified problems but committed to solutions."

As they moved to the collaborative problem-solving portion of the meeting, the energy remained high. Jason raised an issue with the charting library they were using. It handled most cases well, but struggled with the complex drill-down requirements in the reporting module.

Again, the team engaged collectively rather than leaving Jason to solve it alone. Dmitri sketched an alternative approach on the whiteboard. Mei shared a similar problem she'd solved on a previous project. Even Victor, not typically involved with UI components, offered a technical insight about data transformation that might simplify the solution.

In fifteen minutes, they'd outlined a viable approach that Jason could implement, drawing on collective experience that no individual possessed alone.

The open forum that concluded the meeting brought unexpected benefits. Thomas, typically reserved, raised a concern about their deployment process that no one had previously recognised as a shared problem. Priya mentioned a requirement change coming from the business team that would affect multiple components. These issues might never have surfaced in their previous status-focused meetings.

As the team filed out, the energy was palpable. Conversations continued into the hallway, with Dmitri and Thomas already discussing implementation details of the automated code checks. Thomas slid the cap back on his marker and deadpanned, "It was smoother this time. Feels like we're finally thinking ahead for once."

"That went well," Mei said, lingering behind with Marcia. "Really well, actually."

"It did," Marcia agreed. "What struck you most about it?"

Mei considered the question. "People weren't just reporting - they were thinking together. And the solutions we developed were better than what any of us would have created individually."

James appeared in the doorway. "How was the new format?" Leading by example with his physical presence, a 'desk visit' of sorts.

"See for yourself," Marcia replied, gesturing to the whiteboard filled with notes, diagrams, and action items. "More productive than I dared hope."

"The true test will be whether these ideas translate into action," James observed.

"True," Marcia acknowledged. "But I'm optimistic. People commit to what they help create."

That optimism proved warranted over the following days. By Friday, Victor had circulated draft standards for code reviews. Thomas had evaluated three automated checking tools and recommended one for implementation. Mei had created a simple but effective rotation system for reviewers.

Most tellingly, Jason's charting issue - which might have lingered for weeks as a solo struggle - was resolved through the collaborative approach they'd developed during the meeting.

The "What's on This Week" email Marcia sent the following Monday highlighted these achievements alongside their regular progress updates. Elizabeth Parker's response was immediate:

This is impressive progress. The code review improvements address quality issues I've been concerned about for months. I'm particularly struck by how quickly you moved from discussion to implementation.

Robert Miller's feedback came through James: "He says whatever you're doing with that team, keep doing it. He hasn't seen this kind of collaborative momentum at Alpha in years."

In anticipation of their second themed meeting on environment standardisation, she reflected on what was making the difference. The new meeting format wasn't just about structuring time differently - it was about creating space for a fundamentally different kind of conversation. Rather than reporting status up to her, team members were engaging directly with each other, combining their diverse perspectives to solve problems no individual could fully address alone.

The communication ecosystem they were building was becoming more than the sum of its parts. Each element reinforced the others, creating a rhythm that aligned individual work with collective purpose.

Thomas stopped by her desk that afternoon with a question about the upcoming meeting. "Will we follow the same format for the environment standardisation discussion?"

"Yes," Marcia confirmed. "It worked well. Though I'm thinking Dmitri might facilitate that portion since he's been leading the research."

Thomas nodded thoughtfully. "That makes sense. He understands the technical requirements best." He hesitated, then added, "The meeting last week was really productive. I've been at Alpha for three years, and it was the first time I felt everyone was truly working toward the same goal."

Coming from the typically reserved Thomas, this was high praise indeed. As he returned to his desk, Marcia added a note to her leadership journal

The right structures don't just organise work - they transform relationships.

The communication tools they'd implemented weren't just making them more efficient - they were making them more connected. And that connection was becoming the foundation for everything else they were achieving together.

✧ ✧ ✧

Before Marcia could celebrate the positive feedback, James appeared at her desk with an unusually serious expression.

"We need to talk. Privately."

In Conference Room B, James closed the door carefully. "I just came from a leadership meeting. There's something you should know. The infrastructure team has proposed taking over the FreshWorks project."

Marcia felt her stomach drop. "What? Why?"

"They claim your team's quality issues and timeline slips warrant a change. Marcus Keller is pushing hard for it." James named the infrastructure team lead, known for his aggressive pursuit of high-visibility projects.

"But we've turned things around -"

"I know. And Robert knows. But Marcus has allies on the executive team. He's positioning this as 'protecting client relationships.'"

Marcia's mind raced. They'd worked so hard to transform, to build trust with Elizabeth. Now it could all be taken away?

"What do I do?" she asked.

James leaned forward. "You demonstrate undeniable value. The visual board, the skills matrix, the documentation - these aren't just nice-to-haves anymore. They're your proof that this team has something no one else does."

"A systematic approach," Marcia realised.

"Exactly. Marcus can promise heroics. You can demonstrate sustainable excellence. Which do you think Elizabeth really wants?"

✧ ✧ ✧

Three weeks into their new communication system, Marcia found herself staring at her calendar with a sinking feeling. Between client meetings, one-on-ones, and an unexpected system issue that had consumed most of Tuesday, she hadn't prepared the "What's on This Week" email that was supposed to go out Monday morning. It was now Wednesday afternoon, and her inbox showed three separate messages from stakeholders asking for status updates.

"So much for consistency," she muttered.

"Everything okay?" Mei asked, stopping by her desk with a steaming mug of tea.

"I dropped the ball on the weekly update," Marcia confessed. "First week I've missed it, but it feels like I've broken a promise."

Mei leaned against the desk. "The team was wondering about that. A few people mentioned missing it during stand-up yesterday."

"Really?" Marcia looked up, surprised that the absence had been noticed so quickly.

"It's become part of our rhythm," Mei explained. "People use it to plan their week, and our stakeholders have stopped sending those random 'just checking in' emails that used to drive everyone crazy."

Marcia sighed, rubbing her temples. "I know. That's why I'm frustrated with myself. The first time we hit turbulence, I let the communication slip."

"Why don't you delegate it?" Mei suggested.

"Delegate?"

"Sure. Make it a rotating responsibility, like we're doing with the themed discussions in our team meetings."

The suggestion was so obvious that Marcia felt a bit foolish for not thinking of it herself. Leadership wasn't about personally handling every task - it was about creating sustainable systems.

"That's brilliant," she said. "Would you be willing to help set it up?"

Fairly quickly, they had created a simple rotation system. Each team member would take turns drafting the weekly update, with Marcia reviewing before sending. A standardised template ensured consistency, while a shared document made it easy to collect input throughout the week rather than scrambling Monday morning.

"I'll take this week's update," Dmitri volunteered unexpectedly when Marcia presented the plan during Thursday's stand-up. "I can send a draft by end of day."

"I'll handle next week," Victor added, further surprising Marcia. The most process-oriented team member had become one of the strongest supporters of their communication systems.

True to his word, Dmitri sent a draft by 4 pm. It was meticulously detailed, capturing progress across all components with technical precision. Marcia made a few small edits to adapt the language for non-technical stakeholders, then scheduled it to send Friday morning with a brief explanation of the delay.

The response was immediate and positive. Elizabeth replied within the hour:

Appreciate the update, even if it's a few days late. The detailed technical status helps me calibrate expectations with our implementation team. Good idea to rotate responsibility - sustainable processes always beat heroic efforts.

Robert Miller's response was characteristically brief but encouraging:

Delegated communication = scalable leadership. Good move.

Perhaps most telling was a message from Sarah in Business Analysis:

Was getting worried when Monday's update didn't arrive! This system has helped us coordinate requirements delivery much more effectively. Glad to see it continuing.

As Marcia headed into the weekend, she reflected on the experience. The missed update had initially felt like a failure, but it had led to something more valuable - a more resilient system that didn't depend on her alone.

Monday morning, she arrived to find Victor already at his desk, composing the weekly update with characteristic precision. He had created a structured form for gathering input and sent it to each team member on Friday afternoon.

"This is impressive," Marcia said, reviewing his draft. "You've made the process even more efficient."

"Logical improvements to reduce friction," Victor replied matter-of-factly. "If the update requires excessive effort, people will resist contributing."

By 9:30 am, the week's update was sent - the most comprehensive and clearly organised yet. The rotation system had not only maintained their communication rhythm but improved it.

The weekly team meeting followed the same pattern. When Marcia caught a flu that kept her home one Wednesday, Mei stepped in to facilitate without missing a beat. The team had internalised the format and valued the outcomes enough to maintain it regardless of who was leading.

"You've achieved something remarkable," James commented during their check-in the following week. "True process adoption."

"What do you mean?" Marcia asked.

"Most new processes depend on their champion," James explained. "They thrive while that person pushes them forward but collapse when attention shifts elsewhere. You've crossed the threshold to self-sustaining systems - the team maintains them because they see the value, not because you're advocating for them."

Marcia considered this. The communication tools they'd implemented - daily stand-ups, weekly updates, and structured team meetings - had indeed become part of the team's operating rhythm. They weren't "Marcia's processes" anymore; they belonged to everyone.

This was most evident in how the team had begun adapting the tools to suit their needs. Victor had refined the weekly update template. Thomas had suggested moving the stand-up location to better accommodate the growing visual task board. Dmitri had proposed a modification to the team meeting format that created more time for technical deep dives when needed.

These weren't deviations from the system - they were evolutionary improvements that showed true ownership.

The proof came in their metrics. Since implementing their communication ecosystem, client satisfaction scores had risen dramatically. Internal coordination issues had decreased by over 60%. And most significantly, the team was now ahead of their revised schedule for the FreshWorks project.

As Elizabeth Parker noted in her monthly review: "The difference isn't just in what you're delivering, but how you're delivering it. The transparency and consistency have rebuilt trust that was severely damaged under previous leadership."

The Friday before his rotation as weekly update author, Jason approached Marcia with an idea. "What if we added a brief section highlighting individual contributions? Not just what components were completed, but who solved particularly challenging problems or went above and beyond?"

"That's a great idea," Marcia agreed. "It recognises people's efforts and helps stakeholders understand the human element behind the work."

When Jason's update went out the following Monday, the new "Team Spotlight" section called out Dmitri's elegant solution to a data transformation challenge and Thomas's extra effort to improve test coverage over the weekend.

The response was immediate - both Elizabeth and Robert specifically mentioned how much they appreciated the personal dimension. More importantly, team members began privately recognising each other's contributions to ensure they were included in future updates.

Six weeks after implementing their first "What's on This Week" email, Marcia found herself in a quarterly review with Robert Miller and other executive leaders. As she presented the FreshWorks project status, Robert interrupted her slide presentation.

"Skip ahead to how you transformed the team," he said. "That's what the other leaders need to hear."

Put on the spot, Marcia closed her prepared slides and spoke candidly about their journey - the team goals that aligned their purpose, the skills matrix that mapped their capabilities, the visual management that made work visible, and the communication ecosystem that tied it all together.

"What stands out," she concluded, "isn't any individual tool, but how they work together as a system. And more importantly, how the team has made them their own."

When she finished, Robert turned to the other executives. "This is the approach I want to see adopted across Alpha. Not the specific tools, necessarily, but the systematic thinking about team effectiveness."

As she left the meeting, Marcia felt a quiet pride - not in her leadership, but in what the team had built together. The communication rhythm they'd established wasn't just transmitting information; it was creating connections, building trust, and enabling collaboration that transcended individual contributions.

That systematic approach was becoming their signature. It was a foundation for everything else they achieved together.

Chapter 9
Process Evolution

Marcia stood at the visual task board, a warm and comforting coffee in hand, studying the patterns that had emerged over the past few weeks. The Enterprise Solutions team had made remarkable progress with their frameworks. The daily stand-ups and weekly meetings were running smoothly, and the 'What's On This Week' email had become an anticipated touchstone for stakeholders.

But something was still missing.

As she traced her finger across the board's colourful cards, she noticed several tasks that seemed hauntingly familiar. Hadn't Thomas fixed that authentication issue three weeks ago? Why was Victor addressing the same database optimisation problem they'd solved in April?

"Noticing a pattern?" James asked, appearing beside her.

"We're solving the same problems repeatedly," Marcia said. "It's like institutional amnesia."

James nodded. "The greatest process improvement gets lost if no one remembers it existed."

"We need documentation," Marcia realised. "Not just project specifications, but process knowledge. How we solved things, not just what we solved."

"Ah, you've reached that stage," James smiled. "Most teams resist documentation until they feel the pain of its absence."

Marcia grimaced. "I'd say we're feeling it. Yesterday Victor spent four hours recreating a database query structure he'd already built for another module. If he'd documented the approach..."

"Time to introduce the next tool," James suggested, tapping her Team Leaders Toolbox folder.

During that morning's stand-up, Marcia observed the team with new awareness. When Dmitri mentioned struggling with a reporting interface issue, Mei quietly noted, "I think Jason solved something similar last month."

"I did?" Jason looked puzzled. "Oh right, for the inventory module. But I don't remember the exact approach."

Later, when Thomas reported that the automated testing framework was throwing unexpected errors, Victor frowned. "That's the same issue we fixed in the authentication module. We should have documented the solution."

As team members returned to their desks, Marcia noticed the frustration lingering in their expressions. They were wasting valuable time and energy rediscovering solutions to problems they'd already solved.

"Can we talk?" she asked, approaching Victor's meticulously organised workspace. "I noticed your comment about documentation during stand-up."

Victor removed one side of his headphones. "It's inefficient to solve identical problems repeatedly. We need a systematic approach to preserving solutions."

"Exactly what I've been thinking," Marcia agreed. "Would you be willing to help design a documentation framework for the team? Something structured but not overly burdensome?"

Victor's expression shifted from mild surprise to interest. "I have ideas about a categorisation system that would balance detail with accessibility."

"Perfect," Marcia said. "Could you sketch something for tomorrow's team meeting? I'd like to make this our next focus."

As she moved through the office, Marcia posed similar questions to each team member. Thomas emphasised the need for troubleshooting guides. Dmitri wanted clear standards for what deserved documentation. Each perspective revealed different needs and concerns.

Mei cleared her throat, her response unusually firm. "What if I... took point on a searchable wiki-style format?" She tapped the edge of her notebook. "I can mock-up an outline tonight so we have something to review at tomorrow's meeting - if that works for you."

"That's perfect, Mei," Marcia said, smiling.

That afternoon, Marcia reviewed the documentation section of her Team Leaders Toolbox. The guide outlined different documentation types: expectations documentation that defined standards and specifications, how-to guides that provided step-by-step instructions, and living documentation that evolved with team learning.

She drafted a simple agenda to present at tomorrow's meeting, focusing on three key questions:

1. *What types of knowledge are we losing?*
2. *What documentation formats would actually be used?*
3. *How do we make documentation a natural part of our workflow?*

Later, passing by the break room, Marcia overheard a conversation that confirmed the urgency of her initiative.

"This is the third time I've had to explain the deployment sequence," Thomas was saying to Jason. "If we just had it written down somewhere."

"I know," Jason replied. "And I spent an hour yesterday showing Priya how to configure the charting library - again."

"Documentation," Thomas said with a sigh. "We always talk about doing it, but somehow it never happens."

Marcia smiled to herself. This time would be different. Unlike previous attempts that treated documentation as an afterthought, she planned to integrate it into their existing systems. The visual task board could track documentation tasks. The skills matrix could identify documentation responsibilities. Their weekly meetings could include documentation reviews.

Returning to her workspace, Elizabeth Parker's latest email contained a question about their approach to data validation - a topic they'd extensively discussed three weeks ago but never formally documented. As Marcia composed a detailed explanation, she realised she was essentially creating documentation on demand, but in a format that wouldn't benefit the rest of the team.

The pattern was clear: without systematic documentation, knowledge remained trapped in individual minds or scattered across emails and chat messages. When team members moved on or focused elsewhere, that knowledge effectively disappeared.

As she finished her day's tasks, Marcia spotted Victor working intently at his desk, sketching what appeared to be an elaborate documentation framework. Nearby, Mei was organising a collection of notes and screenshots about user interface patterns the team had developed.

The motivation was there. People understood the problem. They just needed a system that made documentation sustainable rather than an additional burden. The needed a framework that captured knowledge as it was created rather than requiring separate effort after the fact.

Tomorrow's meeting would be their chance to put such a system in place, transforming individual frustration into collective action. Just as they'd done with the other tools, they would tackle documentation as a shared challenge with a systematic solution.

The team that had learned to make work visible would now learn to make knowledge persistent.

✧ ✧ ✧

"Documentation shouldn't be a burden - it should be a relief," Marcia began, standing before the whiteboard in Conference Room B. The team had gathered for their weekly meeting, curiosity evident on their faces as they noticed the topic: "Making Knowledge Persistent."

"Yesterday, I asked each of you about documentation needs," she continued. "The consensus was clear: we're solving the same problems repeatedly because our solutions aren't being captured."

Heads nodded around the table. Even Victor, typically reserved with expressions of agreement, gave a deliberate nod.

"Before I share my thoughts, I'd like to hear from Victor, who's been working on a potential framework."

Victor rose and approached the whiteboard with surprising eagerness. He uncapped a marker and began sketching a structured diagram.

"I propose a three-tier knowledge management system," he explained, his voice more animated than usual. "First tier: quick references for common procedures - deployment steps, environment setup, troubleshooting sequences. Second tier: solution patterns that can be applied across multiple contexts. Third tier: architectural decisions with rationales."

The team leaned forward, engaged by the clarity of Victor's vision. He continued explaining his categorisation system, complete with naming conventions and cross-referencing suggestions.

"What's most important," he concluded, "is that documentation becomes part of our definition of 'done.' No task is complete until its solution is properly recorded."

A brief silence followed as the team absorbed his proposal. Then, unexpectedly, Dmitri spoke up.

"This would have saved me countless hours," he admitted. "Last week I struggled with a data transformation pattern that Victor had already solved."

"The challenge," Thomas interjected, "is making time for documentation when we're under pressure to move to the next task."

Marcia nodded. "That's exactly why we need to integrate documentation into our existing systems rather than treating it as a separate activity."

She moved to the whiteboard and added to Victor's diagram, showing how documentation tasks could be represented on their visual board, how weekly updates could include documentation progress, and how their skills matrix could identify documentation ownership.

"I'm thinking we start small," she suggested. "Each of you identify one process or solution pattern you've developed that would benefit others. We'll create a template based on Victor's framework and document those first six items as a pilot."

"Where will we store these?" Marcia asked practically.

"I've set up a wiki on our SharePoint," Mei replied. "It's searchable, supports categories, and allows collaborative editing."

Jason had been doodling in his notebook margins, but suddenly he stopped and looked up. Instead of his usual hesitance, his hand shot up with quiet confidence, "What about stuff that changes? Some of our processes are still evolving."

"That's why we call it 'living documentation'," Marcia smiled. Mei added, "The wiki tracks versions and shows when content was last updated. We can review and refresh documentation during our regular meetings."

The conversation flowed energetically as team members began calling out processes they wanted to document. Thomas mentioned his testing framework setup. Mei described UI patterns for responsive displays.

What struck Marcia most was the enthusiasm. Unlike previous meetings where documentation was met with reluctant sighs, the team now approached it with almost eager anticipation. The difference? They'd felt the pain of knowledge lost and were motivated to prevent it happening again.

"Let's make this concrete," Marcia said, checking her watch. "We have twenty minutes left. What if we draft our first document right now, together? It can serve as a template for the others."

Agreement rippled through the room. After brief discussion, they settled on documenting the deployment process, which everyone agreed was both essential and frequently misremembered.

Marcia opened the wiki on the room's display. "Let's build this together. Thomas, since you handle most deployments, can you walk us through while I type?"

What followed was one of the most collaborative sessions Marcia had witnessed. Thomas outlined the deployment steps while others chimed in with clarifications and edge cases. Victor suggested logical groupings. Mei proposed adding screenshots at key decision points. Even Priya, who rarely spoke in technical discussions, offered valuable perspective about business validation steps.

Within fifteen minutes, they'd created a high-level deployment guide that captured not just the steps but the rationale behind them and common pitfalls to avoid.

"This is amazing," Marcia said, scrolling through the draft document. "And it took us less time than Thomas usually spends explaining the process to someone who's forgotten it."

"The real test will be whether people actually use it." Dmitri noted pragmatically.

"Fair point," Marcia acknowledged. "So let's make it impossible to ignore. I'll print laminated quick-reference versions for workstations. We'll link it from the task board for deployment tasks. And most importantly, we'll reference it during stand-ups instead of re-explaining processes."

As the meeting concluded, Marcia assigned each team member to document their chosen process before the next weekly meeting, using the deployment guide as a template.

"This feels different from past documentation attempts," Mei commented as they filed out of the conference room. "It's not just busy work - it's solving a real problem we all experience."

"That's the key," Marcia replied. "Documentation works when it serves the documenters, not just future readers."

The next morning, Marcia arrived to find something unexpected: Victor had already completed his documentation on database query optimisation patterns. More surprising still, he'd gone beyond his assignment to create a detailed template structure for future documents, complete with sections for context, solution approach, code examples, and lessons learned.

"This is fantastic," Marcia told him, reviewing his work. "Would you mind if I share your template with the rest of the team?"

Victor looked pleased. "That was my intention. Standardisation improves usability."

By lunchtime, Marcia noticed team members huddled around Thomas's desk, watching as he added his testing framework documentation to the wiki. There was an energy to their interaction that transcended mere obligation - they were genuinely engaged in preserving and sharing their collective knowledge.

✧ ✧ ✧

Elizabeth Parker stopped by that afternoon for a project update. As Marcia walked her through recent progress, she mentioned their documentation initiative.

"I'd like to see that," Elizabeth said. "Documentation has been a persistent gap in previous Alpha projects."

Marcia showed her the wiki with its growing collection of guides. "We're starting small, focusing on high-value processes that get frequently forgotten."

Elizabeth reviewed the deployment document with evident approval. "This addresses one of my biggest frustrations - inconsistent deployment practices. Would you mind if our implementation team borrowed this approach? We have similar knowledge management challenges."

"Not at all," Marcia replied. "The templates are designed to be adaptable."

Marcia pulled out a single laminated page. "Let me show you more broadly the structured approach we actually use."

She placed the document on the table - a one-page summary of the Team Leaders Toolbox 4 Essential Tools. A visual of how team goals, skills matrix, roadmap and resource allocation plan come together for leading teams, connected by arrows, with simple icons and brief descriptions.

"This is it?" Elizabeth asked, surprised. "This is what transformed your team?"

"The tools are simple," Victor said, having joined the impromptu presentation. "The transformation comes from consistent application and systematic evolution."

Mei added, "Each tool reinforces the others. Goals give direction, the skills matrix optimises capability, visual management creates transparency, and continuous improvement prevents stagnation."

Elizabeth leaned forward, studying the simple diagram. "Could we use this with our other vendors?"

"The beauty is its adaptability," Marcia explained. "These aren't rigid prescriptions. They're frameworks that teams shape to their needs."

Marcia handed Elizabeth the laminated page. "You can take this copy."

Elizabeth asked, "Could you walk our project managers through this?"

As Marcia agreed to facilitate a workshop for FreshWorks' internal teams, she caught James's eye. He gave her a subtle nod - she'd just transformed their internal tools into something with strategic value beyond Alpha's walls.

Later, James would tell her this moment - when she presented their toolbox not as theory but as lived practice - was when he knew she was ready for the Practice Lead role.

As Elizabeth left, Marcia reflected on how their internal improvement was already creating ripple effects beyond the team. What had begun as a solution to their own frustrations was becoming a model that others might follow.

The documentation system, like their other tools, was more than a static artifact - it was a living framework that would grow and evolve with the team's needs. They had taken a first step toward becoming a learning organisation that preserved and built upon its collective wisdom.

✧　✧　✧

"And that's how we structure our daily stand-ups," Marcia explained, pointing to the visual task board where the team would gather in fifteen minutes. "Any questions so far, Andrea?"

The newest member of the Enterprise Solutions team - a front-end developer with four years of experience - shook her head, looking slightly overwhelmed but determined. "It's a lot to take in, but everything seems well-organised."

Marcia smiled sympathetically. "First days are always information overload. But don't worry - we have documentation for all of this."

At the mention of documentation, Andrea's expression brightened with surprise. "Really? At my last job, onboarding was basically 'follow someone around until you figure it out.'"

"We used to be the same way," Marcia offered as they walked toward Andrea's new workspace. "But we learned the hard way that tribal knowledge doesn't scale. Now we have - "

"The wiki!" Andrea exclaimed, noticing her monitor's open browser tab displaying the team's knowledge base. "Someone set this up already?"

"Victor did," Marcia explained. "He created an onboarding pathway that walks you through all our essential processes in logical order. He's detail oriented."

That was an understatement. In the two weeks since their documentation initiative began, Victor had transformed from reluctant participant to enthusiastic architect of their knowledge management system. His natural affinity for structure and categorisation had found perfect expression in organising the team's collective wisdom.

"This is incredible," Andrea said, scrolling through the comprehensive guides. "At my last job, it took me three months to learn all their unwritten rules."

"You'll still have questions - documentation can't cover everything," Marcia cautioned. "But it gives you a foundation to build on."

As they returned to the team's task board area, Marcia noticed several team members already gathering for stand-up. Dmitri was updating his task cards on the visual board, while Mei was showing Thomas something on her tablet.

"Everyone, this is Andrea Rivera, our new front-end developer," Marcia announced. "Andrea, you already met Victor and Mei during your interviews. This is Dmitri, Thomas, Jason, and Priya."

The team welcomed Andrea warmly. Mei immediately offered to be her "wiki buddy" for the first week, helping navigate their documentation system.

"Perfect timing," Mei said. "We're about to start stand-up, which will give you a good overview of the current project."

As the stand-up began, Marcia watched Andrea carefully. New team members typically spent their first stand-up looking confused as unfamiliar project terminology and inside references flew past them. But Andrea followed along with surprising ease, occasionally glancing at her tablet where she'd opened relevant wiki pages.

When it came Andrea's turn, she spoke confidently: "Today I'll be setting up my development environment using the documentation, then reviewing the UI components library that Jason created. I don't have any blockers yet, but I'm sure I'll find some."

The team chuckled appreciatively at her honesty.

After stand-up, Marcia noticed something remarkable: instead of the typical first-day scenario where a senior team member abandoned their work to help the newcomer set up, Andrea settled at her desk and began following the environment setup guide independently. Nearby, Victor continued his scheduled work, occasionally glancing over to ensure Andrea was progressing.

By lunchtime, Andrea had completed her environment setup and was exploring the codebase - a process that had typically taken new hires a full day or more of trial and error.

"How's it going?" Marcia asked, stopping by Andrea's desk.

"Surprisingly well," Andrea replied. "The documentation is extremely thorough. I've only had to ask Victor two questions so far."

Victor, overhearing from his adjacent desk, turned slightly. "The wiki eliminated 93% of the questions new team members typically ask on their first day, based on my observations of previous onboarding experiences."

Marcia suppressed a smile at his precise calculation but appreciated the sentiment. Their documentation efforts were clearly paying dividends already.

Later that afternoon, James wandered over to Marcia's desk. "I hear the new team member is having an unusually smooth first day."

"Word travels fast," Marcia observed.

"Good news always does," James replied. "Robert mentioned it after his meeting with HR. Apparently Andrea sent an enthusiastic email to her recruiter about the onboarding experience."

Marcia raised her eyebrows in surprise. "Already? She's only been here half a day."

"That's exactly why it made an impression," James said. "Most new hires spend their first day feeling lost and overwhelmed. Yours is already productive."

As they spoke, Marcia noticed Andrea and Jason engaged in an animated conversation about UI component architecture. Andrea was pointing to documentation on her screen while suggesting refinements to their approach - contributing value on her very first day.

"The documentation system is exceeding my expectations," Marcia enthused. "It's not just preserving knowledge - it's accelerating our ability to integrate new perspectives."

James nodded thoughtfully. "Documentation is often viewed as a historical record - capturing what was done. But effective documentation is a springboard - enabling what comes next."

Nearing the end of the day, Andrea had not only completed her environment setup but had submitted her first small code change - a fix to a UI rendering issue she'd discovered while exploring the system. The pull request included updated documentation noting the issue and solution.

Andrea hesitated at the edge of Marcia's workspace, shifting her weight from foot to foot. She'd been the new person before, always careful not to overstep. But something about this team felt different. She took a small breath and stepped forward - not just physically, but into a sense of belonging she hadn't expected to find so quickly.

"I hope you don't mind," Andrea told Marcia as they wrapped up her first day. "I noticed the fix wasn't documented and thought it might save someone else time in the future."

"Mind? That's exactly the culture we're trying to build," Marcia assured her. "Documentation isn't just for onboarding - it's an ongoing habit."

After Andrea left, Marcia took a moment to wander through the team area, observing the subtle but significant changes that had occurred over the past weeks. Thomas was updating testing documentation as he completed his current task. Dmitri had created a troubleshooting decision tree for database connectivity issues. Even Priya, initially the most reluctant documenter, was cataloguing business rule exceptions she'd discovered.

The momentum was building - each positive experience reinforcing the value of their documentation efforts. What had started as a solution to recurrent problems was evolving into a fundamental shift in how they worked. By reducing the cognitive load of remembering procedures and rediscovering solutions, they were freeing mental energy for more creative thinking.

Marcia returned to her desk and opened her leadership journal, noting the day's observations. *Systematic documentation approach not just preserving knowledge, but creating space for innovation.*

Andrea's experience had demonstrated the power of documentation not just for existing team members, but for expanding their collective capability. It was growing a foundation upon which they could build with increasing speed and confidence.

✧ ✧ ✧

The afternoon sunlight slanted through the office windows as Marcia returned from her meeting with Elizabeth Parker. The client review had gone exceptionally well - Elizabeth had specifically praised the team's improved consistency and knowledge sharing. As Marcia approached the Enterprise Solutions area, something unusual caught her eye.

Victor was standing at the whiteboard, surrounded by several team members. This wasn't his typical behaviour - Victor generally avoided impromptu gatherings, preferring scheduled interactions with clear agendas. Yet here he was, marker in hand, explaining something with uncharacteristic animation.

Marcia slowed her pace, observing from a distance. On the whiteboard, Victor had drawn an intricate diagram of what appeared to be the authentication system architecture. Andrea, now in her second week with the team, was asking questions that Victor answered with surprising patience. Thomas and Dmitri contributed occasional insights, while Jason took photos of the evolving diagram with his phone.

"Are you documenting this?" Marcia heard Andrea ask.

"Of course," Victor replied, as if the question were unnecessary. "I'm transferring the diagram to the wiki after this session, with expanded annotations on each component."

Marcia felt a small thrill of satisfaction. Victor - who had initially viewed documentation as a distraction from 'real work' - was now voluntarily documenting complex systems without any prompting.

She approached the group. "Looks like I missed something interesting."

"Victor's explaining the authentication architecture," Andrea said. "I had questions about how it connects to the reporting module, and instead of just giving me a quick answer..."

"Quick answers create knowledge gaps," Victor interjected. "The system has internal logic that becomes clear when properly documented."

Thomas nodded in agreement. "Victor's diagram helped me understand why certain test cases keep failing. I've been focusing on the wrong integration points."

Marcia noticed something remarkable about this interaction. It wasn't just Victor sharing knowledge - it was a collaborative exploration. Thomas had identified testing implications. Dmitri had suggested database optimisations. Jason had noted UI considerations. What had begun as a simple question had evolved into a cross-functional understanding that benefited everyone.

"Will you add this to the wiki today?" Marcia asked.

"It's already in progress," Victor confirmed. "I started the basic structure this morning and will complete it with insights from this discussion."

As the impromptu session wrapped up, team members drifted back to their desks with renewed purpose. Marcia lingered with Victor as he carefully photographed his whiteboard work.

"This is impressive," she said. "Not just the diagram, but the initiative you've taken with documentation."

Victor considered her comment with his typical thoroughness. "I've calculated that documenting complex systems reduces related support questions by approximately 74%. The time investment produces a positive return within 2.4 weeks."

Marcia smiled at his precise analysis. "So it's a matter of efficiency?"

"Initially," Victor admitted. "But there's an unexpected benefit." He paused, seeming to search for the right words. "When I document systems, I discover flaws in my own understanding. The process forces clarification."

This insight surprised Marcia. She had anticipated the efficiency argument, but not this recognition of personal growth.

"Plus," Victor added, "it's... satisfying... to create order from complexity."

Later that afternoon, Marcia visited their wiki to find Victor had already uploaded his authentication system documentation. It was remarkably comprehensive - not just technical details, but design rationales, historical context, and connections to other system components. More impressive still, he'd created templates for other architectural documentation, making it easier for team members to follow his example.

But what truly caught Marcia's attention was a new section Victor had added entitled "Future Considerations." Here, he had thoughtfully documented potential scaling challenges and recommended approaches for addressing them - providing foresight that would benefit the team long after the current project ended.

This wasn't just documentation - it was legacy building.

At her desk, Marcia reflected on the transformation she'd witnessed. The documentation initiative had begun as a pragmatic solution to recurring problems, but it had evolved into something much more significant. It had become a vehicle for deeper understanding, cross-functional collaboration, and professional growth.

Their documentation system now functioned as a living knowledge base that captured not just what they did, but why they did it - preserving context and rationale that would otherwise be lost over time.

James appeared at her desk. "I heard Victor gave an impromptu architecture lesson today."

"Complete with comprehensive documentation," Marcia confirmed. "Without any prompting from me."

James nodded appreciatively. "That's when you know a process has truly taken hold - when people drive it themselves because they see the value."

"It's spread beyond just capturing procedures," Marcia observed. "They're documenting design decisions, architectural patterns, even future considerations. It's becoming part of how they think, not just what they do."

"That's the evolution of any successful process," James said. "It starts as a deliberate practice, then becomes a habit, and finally transforms into a cultural value."

As they spoke, Marcia noticed other small signs of this cultural shift throughout the team area. Andrea was adding her own notes to a UI component guide. Thomas was recording edge cases he'd discovered during testing. Mei and Priya were collaboratively documenting business rule exceptions.

The barrier between "doing the work" and "documenting the work" had dissolved. Documentation had become an integral part of the work itself - a natural extension of professional pride rather than an administrative burden.

"Next step is reviewing how our documentation connects to our other processes," Marcia told James. "I want to ensure our entire system works as a cohesive whole."

James smiled. "Continuous improvement - the process of improving processes."

As Friday afternoon approached, Marcia gathered her notes for the team retrospective. They had reached a natural milestone - not just in their documentation practices, but in their overall evolution as a team.

Their journey wasn't complete. There were still gaps to address, refinements to make, and new challenges to face. But with each systematic improvement, they were building not just better software, but a better way of working together.

The retrospective would be an opportunity to acknowledge that progress and identify their next evolution - continuing the cycle of improvement that had transformed them from a group of talented individuals into a truly exceptional team.

Chapter 10
Looking Forward

"We've got a problem," Dmitri announced as he entered Marcia's cubicle, tablet in hand. His normally stoic expression carried a hint of genuine concern.

Marcia looked up from her computer. "What kind of problem?"

"A planning problem." He placed his tablet on her desk, displaying a complex project timeline. "We've made excellent progress with our current processes, but we're approaching a decision point for the next phase of FreshWorks."

Marcia studied the timeline with growing unease. The team had spent the past weeks focusing on immediate improvements - team goals, skills matrix, visual management, documentation. These systems had transformed their day-to-day operations, but their planning still focused primarily on the near term.

"I see what you mean," she said, scrolling through the document. "We've been making tactical decisions without a clear long-term strategy."

Dmitri nodded. "Elizabeth asked about our approach to phased deployment yesterday. I realised I couldn't give her a confident answer because we haven't mapped it out beyond the next six weeks."

The realisation landed with surprising weight. For all their improvement in execution, they were still navigating without a complete map.

Marcia glanced at her Team Leaders Toolbox folder. The next section was titled "Roadmap Planning," and while they had a rolling, six-week, look-ahead schedule, they still lacked a longer-term roadmap. Dmitri's concern made it clear that "soon" needed to become "now."

"You're right," she told him. "We need a more comprehensive roadmap. Not just delivery dates, but a vision for how all the pieces fit together over time."

Dmitri seemed relieved by her response. "It would help us make better architectural decisions. Some of the choices we're making now will have long-term implications."

"Let's bring this up at today's stand-up," Marcia suggested. "I think it's time for us to zoom out and look at the bigger picture."

At the morning stand-up, Marcia waited until everyone had shared their updates before addressing the team.

"Dmitri raised an important point this morning," she began. "We've gotten really good at managing our immediate work with the visual board and daily check-ins. But we're making decisions that will affect us months from now without a clear roadmap to guide us."

Marcia pointed to the task board. "This shows us where we are now, but not where we're going or how everything connects over time."

Victor nodded immediately. "I've had similar concerns. Our architectural decisions should be guided by a longer-term vision, not just immediate requirements."

"And from a testing perspective," Thomas added, "I need to know what's coming to properly design my validation approach."

Even Andrea, still new to the team, raised her hand. "At my previous company, the lack of roadmapping led to a complete UI redesign six months into development. Nobody had mapped out how all the user flows would eventually connect."

The energy in the room shifted as team members began discussing instances where a clearer long-term view would have prevented rework or improved decisions.

"I think we've found our next improvement area," Marcia said when the conversation naturally paused. "We need to create a roadmap that shows not just what we're building, but how and when it all comes together."

"Who typically creates roadmaps?" Mei asked. "Is that something you'll develop for us?"

Marcia shook her head. "Like everything else we've implemented, this needs to be a collaborative effort. I can provide a framework, but we need all of your expertise to build a meaningful roadmap."

She outlined her plan: they would dedicate Friday's team meeting to initial roadmap development, with pre-work for everyone to consider their component timelines and dependencies.

"By the end of this week, we should have at least a draft roadmap extending through the complete FreshWorks delivery and beyond," she explained. "Then we can refine it together over the following week."

As everyone drifted back to their desks, Marcia noticed a mix of emotions: excitement about gaining clarity, but also uncertainty about the process. Roadmapping would require them to make commitments and predictions beyond their usual comfort zone.

Making space on her desk, she opened the Roadmap Planning section of her toolkit. James had provided a simple but effective framework - a quarterly view that balanced detail with flexibility, capturing major milestones without overcommitting to specific dates too far in advance.

James strolled over casually shortly after lunch. "I hear you're moving into roadmap territory," he said, leaning against her desk.

"Your grapevine is working well," Marcia replied with a smile. "Dmitri pointed out our planning gap this morning."

"Perfect timing," James said. "Teams typically need roadmapping when they've mastered the basics of daily and weekly management. It's the natural next step in your evolution."

"I'm a bit concerned about getting everyone's input without creating a planning nightmare," Marcia shared, feeling some anxiety. "Everyone sees the roadmap from their own perspective."

James nodded. "That's actually the value - integrating those perspectives into a unified vision. Start with a simple framework and let the team fill in the pieces together."

"Any other advice?" Marcia asked.

"Remember that a roadmap serves multiple audiences," James replied. "For the team, it provides direction and context for daily decisions. For stakeholders, it sets expectations and demonstrates thoughtful planning. For you as a leader, it's a tool to ensure you're allocating resources effectively for both short and long-term needs."

Marcia spent the afternoon developing a roadmap template and planning Friday's session. She created a simple structure with quarters across the top and key workstreams down the left side, leaving plenty of space for the team to fill in milestones and dependencies.

That evening, she sent an email to the team explaining the roadmap concept and asking each person to consider three questions before Friday:

1. *What are the major milestones for your area of responsibility?*
2. *What dependencies do you have on other team members or external groups?*
3. *What decisions need to be made now that will affect your work three or more months from now?*

The responses began arriving within minutes - a promising sign of engagement. Victor sent a detailed timeline of authentication system developments. Thomas outlined his testing milestone strategy. Mei shared UI component evolution plans.

Reviewing their input, Marcia realised how much collective foresight existed within the team. They weren't just focused on immediate tasks; they were thinking ahead in their individual domains. What they lacked was a unified view that connected these individual plans into a coherent whole.

On Thursday, Elizabeth Parker called to discuss the upcoming client review.

"I'd like to see where you're heading with the next phases," she said. "Not just the immediate deliverables, but the complete journey."

"Perfect timing," Marcia replied. "We're developing our comprehensive roadmap this week. I'll have a draft to share with you by Monday."

As Marcia prepared for the roadmapping session, she reflected on how far they'd come. Three months ago, they were a fragmented group struggling with basic coordination. Now they were ready to tackle strategic planning as a unified team.

The roadmap wouldn't just show where they were going - it would demonstrate how deeply their transformation had taken root. They were creating the foundation for longer-term success.

Friday's session would be a significant test of their collective capabilities. But Marcia felt confident that the team had developed the trust, communication skills, and shared understanding necessary to rise to the challenge.

✧ ✧ ✧

Friday morning arrived with an energy that felt different from their usual end-of-week atmosphere. As team members filtered into the large conference room, Marcia noticed they carried notebooks, tablets, and even printed timelines - evidence of the preparation she'd requested.

She'd transformed the space for their roadmapping session, pushing tables against the walls and covering one entire wall with butcher paper marked with a timeline grid. Coloured sticky notes, markers, and string for showing dependencies sat ready on a side table.

"This looks serious," Jason commented, eyeing the setup.

"Planning our future usually is," Marcia replied with a smile. "But it doesn't have to be painful."

Once everyone had arrived, Marcia began. "We've gotten really good at managing our day-to-day work. The visual board shows us where we are now. But we need to connect today's efforts to our longer-term journey."

With a quick gesture to the timeline on the wall. "This roadmap will give us that bigger picture. It's not just about dates - it's about how all our work fits together over time."

Victor, who had positioned himself near the timeline, nodded approvingly. "A systematic view of temporal dependencies is essential for optimal architecture decisions."

"What Victor said," Mei added with a gentle laugh. "But in human speak: knowing what's coming helps us build things right the first time."

Marcia outlined the simple framework she'd created: quarters across the top, key workstreams down the left side, with space to fill in milestones and connections.

"We'll start by mapping what we know for certain," she explained. "Then we'll add the less defined elements, being honest about areas of uncertainty."

Thomas raised his hand. "How far into the future should we plan? At some point, we're just guessing."

"Good question," Marcia acknowledged. "We'll go detailed for the next quarter, broader for the following two quarters, and just major milestones beyond that. The near-term needs to be specific, but the distant future can be directional."

With the approach clear, they began work. Each team member added their major milestones to the timeline using color-coded sticky notes - blue for development, green for testing, yellow for design, pink for business decisions.

As the wall filled with colourful markers of future work, patterns began to emerge. Clusters formed around key delivery dates. Gaps appeared where planning had been vague. Dependencies became visible as they connected related items with string.

"I'm seeing an issue," Dmitri said after about twenty minutes, pointing to a cluttered section in the second quarter. "We've scheduled three major components to integrate at once. That's an enormous testing burden."

Thomas stepped closer, frowning. "I hadn't realised these would all converge. That's a risk we should address now."

Marcia watched as the team naturally began problem-solving, reshuffling priorities and proposing alternative sequencing approaches. This was exactly what she'd hoped for - collaborative planning that surfaced issues while they were still easy to address.

Victor, who had been quietly studying the emerging roadmap, suddenly spoke. "There's a fundamental architecture decision we need to make by next month." He pointed to a junction point where several components connected. "If we choose microsystems here, it affects everything that follows. If we stay with the monolithic approach, we optimise for speed but sacrifice future flexibility."

The team gathered around this critical decision point, discussing technical trade-offs with surprising depth. What struck Marcia was how the physical timeline helped everyone see connections they might have missed in abstract discussions.

"This is why roadmapping matters," she noted as the conversation reached a natural pause. "We're making decisions today that set our direction for months to come."

By lunchtime, they had a draft roadmap that revealed both their detailed near-term plans and their directional future. More importantly, they'd identified several critical decision points that needed immediate attention.

"Let's take a break," Marcia suggested. "When we come back, we'll focus on three things: risks to the roadmap, resource needs over time, and communication strategy for stakeholders."

As the team left for lunch, Marcia remained behind, studying their creation. The timeline revealed a story of increasing capability - initial components giving way to integrated systems, technical foundations enabling richer features.

James appeared in the doorway. "How's it going?"

"Pleasantly surprising," Marcia replied. "They didn't just plot dates - they're having substantive discussions about strategic decisions."

James walked along the timeline, nodding appreciatively. "This is good work. They're thinking like a product team, not just a delivery team."

"What's the difference?" Marcia asked.

"Delivery teams focus on completing assigned tasks. Product teams consider the complete lifecycle and user experience," James explained. "Your team is evolving from 'building it right' to 'building the right things in the right sequence.'"

After lunch, the energy remained high as they tackled the remaining aspects of roadmap planning. The risk discussion proved particularly valuable, with each team member highlighting potential obstacles in their areas.

"We should mark these directly on the roadmap," Victor suggested, producing red dot stickers. "Visual identification of risk factors enables proactive management."

They placed red dots next to high-risk milestones, adding notes about mitigation strategies. This simple visualisation made their challenges explicit rather than hidden.

As they discussed resource allocation across the timeline, patterns emerged that hadn't been obvious before.

"We have three UI-heavy phases in a row," Mei observed, pointing to a stretch in the second quarter. "That puts a lot of pressure on the front-end team, especially with Andrea still ramping up."

"And here," Thomas added, indicating a later section, "we have minimal testing load followed by an intense verification period. That's inefficient."

Andrea, who had been relatively quiet during much of the session, suddenly spoke up. "At my previous company, we addressed similar patterns by creating more balanced feature slices. Instead of completing all back-end, then all front-end work, we delivered vertical slices of functionality."

The team considered this approach, discussing how it might smooth their resource demands while delivering value earlier.

As the afternoon progressed, their roadmap evolved from a simple timeline into a strategic planning tool - showing not just what they would deliver, but how they would approach the journey.

"We need to consider onboarding and training here," Dmitri pointed out, indicating a section where new technologies would be introduced. "That requires advance preparation."

Victor, absorbed with meticulously annotating the roadmap with architectural decision points, added a section for knowledge development alongside the delivery timeline.

By late afternoon, they had created something far more valuable than a simple schedule. Their roadmap captured shared understanding of their path forward, critical decision points, risks, resource needs, and learning requirements.

"This is exceptional work," Marcia told the team as they gathered for a final review. "But remember - a roadmap is a living document, not a fixed prediction. We'll revisit and adjust this regularly as we learn and as conditions change."

As team members began to gather their things, Marcia noticed something remarkable. They weren't just leaving - they were taking photos of the roadmap, continuing discussions about specific sections, making notes for follow-up conversations.

"I need to reconsider my component architecture based on what I learned today," Victor told Dmitri as they headed toward the door. "The integration sequence changes my approach."

Elizabeth Parker called just as Marcia was documenting the day's outcomes.

"How did the roadmap planning go?" she asked.

"Extremely well," Marcia replied. "We've created a comprehensive timeline with identified risks and decision points. I'll have a formalised version to you on Monday."

"Perfect. The executive team is particularly interested in how you're balancing immediate delivery with strategic positioning."

"That's been a central theme of our discussion," Marcia assured her. "The team has shown impressive foresight about technical foundations and future flexibility."

After the call, Marcia carefully photographed every section of their wall-sized roadmap. Tomorrow she would transfer this into a digital format that could be easily shared and updated, but she wanted to preserve the raw collaborative output.

James paused by her desk as she was finishing. "Successful day?"

"Beyond my expectations," Marcia replied. "They grasped the concept immediately and took it further than I anticipated. They're not just plotting delivery dates - they're planning their evolution as a team."

"That's the real power of roadmapping," James observed. "It shifts perspective from the immediate to the eventual. Daily work becomes part of a larger journey."

As Marcia gathered her materials to leave, she reflected on how far they'd come. The roadmap was visible evidence of their transformation from a tactical delivery team to a strategic product team, capable of building for both today's needs and tomorrow's possibilities.

✧　✧　✧

"I think we're missing something important," Mei said, pausing at Marcia's desk, Monday morning takeout coffee in hand.

Marcia looked up from her computer where she'd been finalising the digital version of their roadmap. "What's that?"

"How we'll develop the skills we need for each roadmap phase." Mei gestured toward the newly printed timeline now displayed prominently on the wall. "We've mapped what we need to deliver and when, but not how we'll build our capabilities to get there."

Marcia sat back, immediately seeing the connection. "You're absolutely right."

The roadmap had revealed ambitious technical goals for the coming quarters - microservices architecture, virtual machine provisioning, enhanced security protocols - all requiring skills their team didn't yet fully possess.

"The skills matrix would help here, wouldn't it?" Mei suggested. "We could map our current capabilities against what the roadmap requires."

"That's brilliant," Marcia said, already reaching for her notebook. "Let's make this our focus for tomorrow's team meeting."

After Mei left, Marcia pulled out the team's skills matrix, studying it with fresh eyes. They'd initially created it to optimise current work assignment, but now she saw its potential as a forward-looking development tool.

She opened a new document and began sketching a framework that overlaid their skills matrix with their roadmap timeline, identifying gaps that would need to be addressed through training, mentoring, or strategic hiring.

James appeared mid-morning. "How's the digital roadmap coming?"

"Good, but Mei just pointed out a critical gap in our planning," Marcia explained. "We've mapped what we need to deliver without addressing how we'll develop the necessary skills."

James nodded appreciatively. "Skills planning - the piece teams often miss until it's too late. What's your approach?"

"I'm creating a capability development plan that connects our skills matrix to the roadmap timeline," Marcia said, showing him her draft. "For each major phase, we'll identify required skills, current team capabilities, and how we'll close the gaps."

"Smart approach," James agreed. "Have you considered learning curves? Some capabilities take weeks to develop, others take months."

That evening, Marcia sent a message to the team asking everyone to review the skills matrix before tomorrow's meeting and identify areas where they personally needed growth to support upcoming roadmap phases.

Tuesday's team meeting began with an energy that had become characteristic of their gatherings - purposeful, collaborative, and increasingly strategic.

"Today we're addressing a critical aspect of our roadmap," Marcia began. "We've outlined what we need to deliver, but not how we'll develop the capabilities to get there."

She displayed the skills matrix on the large screen, with color-coding highlighting high, medium, and low proficiency levels across the team.

"Next to it, I've listed key capabilities required for each roadmap phase," she continued. "The gaps between what we need and what we have represent our development challenges."

Victor, ever analytical, immediately spotted patterns. "There's a significant disparity between our current service-oriented architecture knowledge and what's required for Q3 deployment."

"And our security protocol expertise is concentrated in just two people," Thomas added. "That's a risk if either becomes unavailable."

As the team analysed the skills landscape, they naturally shifted from problem identification to solution development. Dmitri suggested an internal knowledge-sharing program. Andrea recommended online courses she'd found valuable. Mei proposed pair programming to spread expertise more evenly.

"We should formalise this," Marcia suggested, moving to the whiteboard. "Let's create a three-part development strategy for each critical skill gap."

She drew three columns:

1. Self-directed learning (courses, documentation, tutorials)
2. Internal knowledge transfer (pair programming, lunch-and-learns, mentoring)
3. External development (formal training, conferences, consultants)

The team enthusiastically populated each column, drawing from their collective experiences to create a comprehensive approach.

"What about skills that none of us currently possess?" Jason asked, pointing to service-oriented architecture integration. "We can't transfer knowledge we don't have."

"That's where we need a pioneer strategy," Marcia explained. "Someone becomes the lead learner, developing that capability first, then sharing with others."

To her surprise, team members immediately began volunteering for pioneer roles. Victor offered to lead security protocol advancement. Mei stepped up for UI performance optimisation. Even Thomas, typically reserved, volunteered to develop advanced automated testing frameworks.

"I'll create a structured template," Dmitri offered unexpectedly. "For each pioneer area, we should document learning resources, milestone targets, and knowledge transfer approaches."

As the conversation evolved, Marcia observed something remarkable: the team wasn't just planning technical development - they were creating a learning ecosystem that would strengthen their collective capabilities.

"There's one more dimension we should consider," Marcia suggested. "Timing. Some skills need to be developed immediately for near-term deliverables. Others can be developed gradually for future phases."

She sketched a simple timeline on the whiteboard, and together they mapped skill development priorities against their roadmap phases, creating a sequenced learning plan that aligned with delivery needs.

By the time they wrapped up the meeting, they had created something far more valuable than a typical training plan. They had developed a comprehensive capability development strategy that connected individual growth with team deliverables.

"This is exactly what we needed," Mei said as they concluded. "Now we're not just hoping we'll have the right skills when we need them - we're systematically developing them."

As the meeting concluded, Marcia noticed something she hadn't anticipated. Rather than returning to their individual tasks, people clustered in small groups discussing learning resources and knowledge-sharing approaches. Victor was showing Dmitri a security framework documentation site. Andrea and Jason were comparing notes on service-oriented architecture courses.

The energy around learning was palpable - not as a separate activity from their "real work," but as an integral part of their professional identity.

Later that day, Marcia polished their capability development plan into a formal document that mapped required skills against the roadmap timeline, with specific development strategies for each area. She shared it with Elizabeth via email.

Elizabeth Parker called that afternoon to discuss the roadmap.

"I'm impressed," she said after Marcia walked her through the updated digital version. "Most teams stop at delivery timelines. You've integrated risk management, resource planning, and now capability development."

"It's been a team effort," Marcia replied. "Everyone's contributing their perspectives."

"That shows," Elizabeth noted.

Noticing Marcia finishing her call while passing, James visited Marcia's desk as he often did. "How did Elizabeth respond to the roadmap?"

"Very positively," Marcia said. "Also, I heard Robert's interested in our capability development approach - he's looking at org-wide skill gaps."

James nodded thoughtfully. "Your team is starting to influence Alpha beyond your immediate project. That's the mark of truly effective leadership - when your approaches become models for others."

As the week progressed, Marcia watched the capability development plan move from concept to action. Victor had already begun his security protocol deep dive, sharing his learning approach with the team. Mei and Andrea had created a UI advancement study group that met during lunch hours. Thomas was researching testing frameworks and documenting his evaluation criteria on the wiki.

The skills matrix that had begun as a tool for optimising current work had evolved into a strategic development framework that connected individual growth with team deliverables.

On Friday afternoon, Marcia updated her leadership journal, reflecting on their journey.

* *Team evolution: basic tools → strategic frameworks*
* *Roadmap = shared vision (team goals made real)*
* *Capability plan = right skills at right time*

* Biggest shift: reactive → proactive mindset
* No longer just "what to do" but "what to learn"
Next focus: integration points?

As she closed her notebook, Marcia spotted Victor and Thomas engaged in an animated discussion about security testing automation - two team members who had barely communicated months ago now collaboratively planning their shared development path.

✧ ✧ ✧

"Is everything ready for the executive review?" Marcia asked, glancing around the conference room where her team was making final preparations.

The large display showed their comprehensive roadmap, now enhanced with their capability development plan. Along the wall, they'd posted printed versions of their team goals, skills matrix, and process documentation - the complete ecosystem of tools they'd implemented over the past few months.

"Just finishing the interactive demonstration," Jason replied, connecting his laptop to the secondary screen. "We'll show how our tools connect from daily execution to long-term strategy."

Mei straightened the printed materials one last time. "Do you think Robert Miller will actually attend? James mentioned he might join."

"James confirmed this morning that he will," Marcia said, trying to keep her voice casual despite the flutter of nervousness she felt. The founder rarely attended project reviews unless they had strategic implications for Alpha Consulting.

The team had come so far since Marcia had stepped into the leadership role. What had begun as emergency intervention for a troubled project had evolved into a systematic transformation of how they worked. Today was their opportunity to showcase not just what they'd delivered, but how they'd fundamentally changed their approach.

Victor arrived, precisely on time as always. "I've prepared additional technical architecture documentation should there be specific questions," he said, placing a neatly organised folder on the table.

"Thanks, Victor. I'm sure it will be helpful," Marcia replied, noting how he'd anticipated potential needs without being asked - another sign of how the team had evolved from reactive to proactive thinking.

At precisely 2:00 pm, the conference room door opened as Robert Miller arrived with Elizabeth Parker and two other executives Marcia recognised from Alpha's leadership team.

"Marcia, good to see you," Robert said, taking the lead. "You know Elizabeth, of course. And I believe you've met Vivian Shah, our new Chief Technology Officer, and Alan Meadows, VP of Delivery."

Marcia greeted each of them, understanding immediately that this was more than a routine project review. The presence of Alpha's CTO and Delivery VP alongside their key client suggested broader organisational interest in their approach.

"Elizabeth was impressed by your team's monthly report and asked for a more detailed overview of your methods," Robert explained. "I thought Vivian and Alan should see it too."

"Let's get started," Elizabeth added with a smile. "I've been telling them how your team has implemented some impressive systems that have transformed your delivery approach."

"Before I begin," Marcia said, "I want to emphasise that what you'll see today represents the collective work of this entire team. These aren't tools I introduced - they're systems we built together - and under the guidance of James Anderson."

She directed attention to the large display. "We'll walk you through our journey from team alignment to strategic planning, showing how each element connects to create a cohesive whole."

For the next twenty minutes, Marcia and her team members took turns explaining their systematic approach. Victor described how the skills matrix optimised work allocation. Mei demonstrated how their visual management system created transparency. Dmitri explained their documentation framework. Thomas showcased their quality improvement processes.

Throughout, Marcia watched the executives' reactions. Elizabeth was nodding appreciatively, already familiar with much of their work. Vivian Shah was taking detailed notes, occasionally asking insightful technical questions. Alan Meadows seemed particularly interested in their resource allocation approach. Robert Miller maintained an inscrutable expression, listening intently but revealing little.

"What impresses me most," Elizabeth commented during a transition, "is how quickly we saw real improvements after these changes. From a client perspective, it's been transformative. Our teams are actually using the features you've delivered instead of finding workarounds. Our executive team has specifically mentioned how much more predictable the rollouts have become. And frankly, my job has gotten significantly easier because I'm no longer constantly explaining delays to our stakeholders."

As they reached the roadmap section, Jason took over, demonstrating the interactive version they'd created. "This isn't just a static timeline," he explained. "It's a living strategic tool that connects daily decisions to long-term objectives."

He zoomed in on the current quarter, showing how their daily and weekly planning tied directly to roadmap milestones. Then he zoomed out to show the bigger picture - how current work laid foundations for future capabilities.

"And here's where things get really interesting," Mei added, taking over. "We've mapped required capabilities against our roadmap phases, creating a development plan that ensures we'll have the skills we need when we need them."

This caught Vivian's attention immediately. "That's precisely what we've been discussing at the executive level - proactive capability development rather than reactive training."

Robert spoke up, offering an exploratory question. "Show us how you identified the skills you'll need for future phases."

Andrea, who had been relatively quiet until now, stepped forward. "We analysed each roadmap milestone, identifying required technical and process capabilities. Then we assessed our current proficiency levels using our skills matrix." She displayed the color-coded gap analysis they'd created. "Red areas represent significant gaps we need to address through training or strategic hiring. Yellow areas need enhancement. Green areas are current strengths."

Robert leaned forward, studying the display with increased interest. "And your approach to addressing the gaps?"

"Three-pronged strategy," Dmitri explained, displaying their development framework. "Self-directed learning, internal knowledge transfer, and external development - sequenced against roadmap milestones to ensure capabilities are in place when needed."

During the following fifteen minutes, the executives asked detailed questions about their approach. How did they balance immediate delivery with capability building? How did they measure skill development progress? How did they integrate new team members into their systems?

The team answered confidently, building on each other's responses - demonstrating not just their processes but their collaborative culture.

When they concluded the formal presentation, Robert addressed the team directly.

"What you've shown today isn't just a project status," he said, his typically reserved demeanour giving way to genuine enthusiasm. "It's a model for how teams should operate across Alpha Consulting."

He turned to the other executives. "This is exactly the systematic approach we've been discussing for our organisational transformation. They've implemented in four months what we've been theorising about for a year."

The praise from Alpha's founder sent a wave of pride through the team, visible in subtle smiles and straightened postures around the room.

"What impressed me most," Vivian added, "is how these tools connect. Your daily work visibly ties to quarterly objectives, which support long-term strategy. That alignment is what we've been trying to create organisation-wide."

After the executives left, the team remained in the conference room, processing what had just happened.

"Did Robert Miller just say we should be a model for the entire company?" Jason asked, sounding slightly stunned.

"He did," Marcia confirmed, unable to suppress her smile. "And he meant it."

"It's logical recognition of systematic excellence," Victor stated matter-of-factly, though Marcia detected a hint of pride in his tone.

"What happens now?" Andrea asked.

"We keep evolving," Marcia replied. "These tools aren't the end point - they're the foundation we'll continue building upon."

As people returned to their desks, James appeared in the doorway.

"I hear the executive review went well," he said with characteristic understatement.

"Better than I could have imagined," Marcia's pride in the achievement showing through in a humble smile. "Robert wants our approach to become a model for other teams."

"I'm not surprised," James said, helping her gather the presentation materials. "You've created something special here. Not just individual tools, but a comprehensive system where each element reinforces the others."

Later that afternoon, James stopped by Marcia's desk again.

"I'm impressed," he said. "Robert rarely shows this level of enthusiasm, and he has asked me to have you document your approach for sharing with other team leaders."

"Happy to," Marcia replied. "Though I should emphasise again - this wasn't my creation. It was truly a team effort - and I couldn't have done it without your guidance and support."

"That's part of what makes it special," James noted. "These aren't imposed processes - they're collaboratively developed systems that everyone has invested in. You took the Team Leader Toolbox notes and evolved them into processes that worked for your team."

As James left, Marcia took a moment to reflect on their journey. Four months ago, she'd stepped into a leadership role she hadn't asked for, facing a fractured team and a troubled project. The transformation since then had exceeded her wildest expectations.

They had evolved from a group of talented individuals into a true team with shared purpose and direction. Their processes had matured from reactive task management to strategic capability development. And most importantly, they had created a system of connected tools that reinforced rather than competed with each other.

Looking across the office, Marcia watched her team at work. Victor was explaining an architectural concept to Andrea, using their documentation wiki as reference. Mei and Thomas were updating the visual board together, discussing testing priorities for the week. Dmitri was quietly adding detail to their capability development plan based on the executives' feedback.

The scene captured everything they'd achieved - not just improved processes but transformed relationships, not just better task management but strategic thinking, and not just individual excellence but collective capability.

As she turned back to her computer to begin documenting their approach for other teams, Marcia felt a deep sense of satisfaction. The journey wasn't over - in many ways, it was just beginning.

Chapter 11
The Perfect Storm

Marcia knew something was wrong the moment she walked into the office on Monday morning. The Enterprise Solutions area, normally buzzing with activity by 8:30 am, was eerily quiet. Empty desks outnumbered occupied ones.

Checking her phone at her desk, she saw a text from Mei: *Down with flu. Doctor says not to come in. Available for a call if absolutely necessary, but feeling terrible.*

Before she could respond, an email notification appeared from Thomas: *Out sick today. Fever and chills. Will try to monitor email.*

And another from Dmitri: *Unable to attend office today due to illness. Available for critical issues only.*

Marcia leaned back and sank lower into her chair, a knot forming in her stomach. Three team members out sick simultaneously - and not just any three, but key people responsible for critical components due this week.

"Perfect timing," she muttered, pulling up their roadmap. FreshWorks was entering a pivotal integration phase where multiple components needed to come together. The schedule had zero flexibility - Elizabeth had confirmed client demonstrations were locked in for Friday.

Victor appeared at her desk, looking as concerned as his typically stoic expression allowed. "We have a staffing problem."

"I noticed," Marcia replied. "Any word from Jason or Andrea?"

"Jason texted that he's running late - childcare issues. Andrea is here but expressing concern about the deployment sequence without Thomas."

Marcia took a deep breath. "Okay, let's assess what this means for our deliverables."

She quickly reviewed their visual task board, grateful they had implemented such clear work visibility. The current status of every component was immediately apparent, including the critical items assigned to their absent team members.

"We have three major deliverables due Thursday," she noted, pointing to the relevant cards. "Mei's UI integration, Thomas's automated testing framework, and Dmitri's reporting module. All in various states of completion, all with dependencies on each other."

Victor nodded. "A significant challenge. However," He paused, seeming to choose his words carefully. "Our documentation and cross-training initiatives may prove valuable in this scenario."

Marcia looked up sharply. He was right. They'd spent weeks building systems that captured knowledge and spread expertise across the team. This would be their first real test of whether those systems worked under pressure.

Jason arrived, looking harried. "Sorry I'm late. What's happening?"

"Perfect storm," Marcia explained, quickly bringing him up to speed. "Half the team is out sick during our most critical integration week."

"Wow," Jason exhaled. "What's the plan?"

"First, let's have an emergency stand-up to reassess priorities," Marcia decided. "Then we'll see if our systems are as good as we think they are."

Fifteen minutes later, the remaining team members gathered around the visual board. The emptiness of the room highlighted their predicament.

"We need to be strategic about this," Marcia began. "We can't simply work harder or longer hours - we need to work smarter using the systems we've built."

She turned to the board. "First, let's identify the truly critical path items that must be completed for Friday's demonstration. Everything else becomes secondary."

Together, they reviewed the in-progress work, ruthlessly prioritising tasks. Three critical components emerged that absolutely could not slip.

"Now, let's assess our capabilities," Marcia continued. "Who can cover what, based on our skills matrix and the documentation we have?"

Andrea spoke up first. "I can handle Mei's UI integration. We pair-programmed on the framework last month, and her documentation is detailed."

"I can continue Dmitri's reporting module," Victor offered, surprising everyone with his willingness to step outside his usual domain. "His process documentation is exceptionally thorough, and I have sufficient database knowledge."

Jason looked concerned. "Thomas's testing framework is the trickiest. None of us have his testing expertise."

"But we have his documentation," Marcia pointed out, pulling up the wiki page Thomas had created. "And he designed it to be usable by non-specialists."

They used the next hour developing a coverage plan, identifying what could be reasonably accomplished and what might need to be modified or deferred. Marcia was impressed by how quickly they adapted, using their skills matrix to identify the best person for each critical task and their documentation to enable smooth handovers.

"I should update Elizabeth," Marcia said as they concluded. "She needs to know about the situation."

"What will you tell her?" Jason asked, concern evident in his voice.

"The truth," Marcia replied. "That we've had an unexpected staffing challenge but have a solid coverage plan using our cross-functional capabilities and knowledge management systems."

Elizabeth's response was measured but supportive: "Staffing issues happen. I'm confident in your team's ability to adapt. Keep me updated on any potential impact to Friday's demonstration."

By lunchtime, they had implemented their coverage plan. Andrea was navigating Mei's UI code with surprising ease, thanks to clear documentation and consistent coding standards. Victor had picked up Dmitri's reporting module work, occasionally referencing the wiki but making steady progress. Jason was cautiously working through Thomas's testing framework, following the detailed procedures he'd documented.

Marcia checked in with each of them, providing support without micromanaging. What struck her most was how their systematic approach to documentation and knowledge sharing was proving its worth in a real crisis.

"This would have been a complete disaster two months ago," she realised. Back then, critical knowledge had been locked in individual team members' heads, and work handovers had been haphazard at best.

Mid-afternoon, James made his way over. "I heard about your staffing challenge. How's it going?"

"I wasn't expecting it to go as well as it has," Marcia admitted. "Everyone's stepped up, and our systems are proving their value. The documentation, skills matrix, visual management - they're all helping us navigate this."

"The true test of any system is how it performs under stress," James observed. "When things are going well, almost any approach can look effective. It's moments like these that separate robust systems from fragile ones."

As the day progressed, Marcia kept communication flowing. She helped the remote sick team members stay informed without pressuring them to work, facilitated quick knowledge transfers when the on-site team hit obstacles, and kept Elizabeth updated on their progress.

By end of day, they had maintained momentum on the critical path items, though at a somewhat reduced pace. The documentation had proven invaluable, enabling team members to pick up unfamiliar work with reasonable efficiency.

As Marcia prepared to leave, she felt cautiously optimistic. They'd survived day one of their perfect storm and had a viable plan for the days ahead. The systems they'd built together were proving their worth precisely when needed most.

Tomorrow would bring new challenges, but they had demonstrated that their team's effectiveness didn't depend solely on individual heroics. The knowledge they'd so carefully captured and shared was carrying them through a crisis that might otherwise have derailed everything.

The perfect storm was testing every aspect of their transformation - and so far, they were weathering it remarkably well.

✧ ✧ ✧

Tuesday morning arrived with mixed news. Thomas texted that he was feeling slightly better and could answer questions remotely, though he wasn't well enough to come in. Mei and Dmitri remained completely out of commission, with Mei's message simply reading: *Still dying. Don't call unless building is on fire.*

"At least we have Thomas available for consultation," Marcia told the small gathering at their morning stand-up. "But we need to continue operating as if we're on our own."

Andrea nodded, looking tired but determined. "I made good progress with Mei's UI components yesterday. The documentation helped, but I hit a few unexpected issues with the responsive layout."

"I encountered similar challenges with the reporting module," Victor added. "Dmitri's documentation covers the standard pathways thoroughly, but lacks detail on exception handling."

Jason rubbed his eyes. "The testing framework is where I'm struggling most. I can follow Thomas's procedures for existing tests, but creating new ones for the integration points is tricky."

Marcia listened carefully, noting how their documentation was performing under real-world pressure. It was working - they were making progress - but the gaps were becoming evident.

"Let's use these insights to improve our documentation going forward," she suggested. "We're discovering exactly where knowledge transfer breaks down."

They agreed on a simple flag system - adding coloured sticky notes to their task board where documentation gaps were causing delays. Red for critical gaps, yellow for minor issues. This would create a visual map of where their knowledge management needed improvement.

As they dispersed to their workstations, Marcia noticed how naturally they had fallen into a problem-solving mindset rather than a blame mindset. No one was complaining about the absent team members or the documentation shortfalls - they were systematically identifying and addressing the gaps.

By mid-morning, the board sprouted several yellow sticky notes and two red ones. The pattern was telling - their process documentation worked well for standard operations but broke down at integration points and exception handling.

Marcia dropped by Jason's desk, where he was struggling with the testing framework. "How's it going?"

"Making progress, but slowly," he admitted. "The documentation assumes a level of testing knowledge I don't have. I keep having to stop and research basic concepts."

"What would make it easier?" Marcia asked.

Jason thought for a moment. "If the documentation included more context - not just what to do but why we're doing it and how it connects to other components."

Marcia nodded, making notes. "That's valuable feedback. Did you ask Thomas about this?"

"I didn't want to bother him when he's sick," Jason said.

"He offered to answer questions," Marcia reminded him. "And your issue is exactly the kind of specific question that's worth asking."

She encouraged Jason to reach out to Thomas with targeted questions rather than struggling alone. Meanwhile, she checked in with Victor, who was making surprisingly good progress on Dmitri's reporting module.

"How are you managing so well with unfamiliar code?" she asked.

Victor, without looking up from his monitor, replied, "The module's architecture follows the patterns we established in our documentation standards. Once I identified the structural similarities, navigation became logical."

Marcia smiled. Victor's observation highlighted an unexpected benefit of their documentation efforts - they weren't just preserving knowledge but creating consistent patterns that made the entire system more understandable.

At Andrea's desk, the situation was more challenging. She had hit a significant roadblock with the UI integration.

"There's a critical user flow that's completely undocumented," she explained, pointing to her screen. "I've tried reverse-engineering from the code, but there are too many possible pathways."

"This seems like a case for remote pair programming," Marcia suggested. "Would Mei be up for a short video call focused just on this specific issue?"

Andrea looked uncertain. "She sounded pretty sick..."

"Let's ask her," Marcia decided. "Keep it focused and time-boxed."

To everyone's surprise, Mei agreed to a fifteen-minute call. From her appearance - pale, wrapped in blankets, barely able to keep her eyes open - she was clearly battling a serious flu. But for those fifteen minutes, she mustered extraordinary focus, walking Andrea through the complex user flow with remarkable clarity.

"You're a lifesaver," Andrea told her before ending the call. "Now go back to sleep."

That brief intervention unblocked Andrea's work, allowing her to make significant progress on the integration. It demonstrated something important: their documentation didn't need to be perfect if they maintained multiple channels of knowledge sharing.

By lunchtime, Elizabeth called for an update.

"We're making steady progress," Marcia reported. "Slower than with our full team, but we're on track for the critical components."

"I'm impressed," Elizabeth admitted. "You're finally making me look good. Keep it up. Most teams would be in crisis mode with half their members out during integration week."

"Thanks Elizabeth, I appreciate your support," Marcia smiled, with a relieved short sharp breath in and long exhale.

After lunch, a new challenge emerged. The integration testing revealed an unexpected compatibility issue between components that had previously worked in isolation.

"This is exactly the kind of edge case that Thomas would spot immediately," Jason lamented, staring at the error messages.

"But we have his testing documentation," Victor pointed out. "Section 3.2 covers integration conflict resolution."

They gathered around Jason's desk, reviewing the relevant documentation. Thomas had indeed documented a systematic approach to diagnosing integration issues, with decision trees for identifying root causes.

Following his methodology step by step, they isolated the conflict to a specific data handling pattern. The fix wasn't obvious, but the diagnostic approach had narrowed the problem space considerably.

"I'll text Thomas with the specific issue," Jason said, now much more confident about asking a targeted question. "This is exactly the kind of high-value use of his limited energy."

Thomas responded within minutes, pointing them to an additional wiki page he'd created but hadn't yet linked to the main documentation. It contained exactly the pattern they needed.

"This is why living documentation is so valuable," Marcia observed. "The knowledge exists, but sometimes the connections aren't obvious."

By end of day, they had overcome the major technical hurdles. They were still behind their ideal schedule, but the critical path items remained on track for Friday's demonstration.

As they wrapped up their daily stand-up, Andrea made an observation that resonated with everyone: "I've learned more about our system in the past two days than in the previous two weeks. Having to rely on documentation forces you to understand things differently."

Victor nodded. "This experience has highlighted systematic improvements needed in our knowledge management approach. We should establish more consistent cross-referencing between related components."

"And include more context and 'why' explanations," Jason added.

Marcia felt a surge of pride in how her team was responding to the crisis - not just surviving it but learning from it, already thinking about how to strengthen their systems further.

As she updated their status in the project management system, she added notes about the documentation gaps they'd identified. These weren't failures but valuable insights that would make their knowledge management more robust.

James stopped by as she was preparing to leave. "How's day two of your perfect storm?"

"Educational," Marcia replied with a tired smile. "Our systems are working - not perfectly, but well enough to keep us moving forward. And we're learning exactly where they need strengthening."

"That's the real value," James observed. "Not just weathering this crisis, but building greater resilience for the next one." James had confidence in Marcia's ability to manage this crisis.

Walking to her car, Marcia reflected on how their systematic approach was proving its worth. The documentation wasn't perfect - no documentation ever could be - but it provided enough structure to keep the team functioning despite significant disruption.

More importantly, the team's mindset had shifted fundamentally. They weren't just passive users of documentation but active contributors to a living knowledge system, already planning how to improve it based on their current experience.

Tomorrow would bring new challenges as they moved deeper into integration, but Marcia felt cautiously optimistic. Their systems were bending under pressure but not breaking.

✧ ✧ ✧

Wednesday morning brought a small reprieve. Mei texted that she was feeling well enough to work remotely for a few hours. Thomas reported his fever had broken, though he was still too weak to come into the office. Only Dmitri remained completely unavailable, his absence now stretching into its third day.

"We're in better shape today," Marcia announced at their morning stand-up, the small team gathered around their visual task board. "But let's not get complacent. We still have significant integration work to complete before Friday's demonstration."

Andrea updated her cards on the board, moving several to the "Done" column. "The UI components are coming together now that Mei can answer questions remotely. But I've discovered something concerning about our deployment process."

"What's that?" Marcia asked.

"It's documented thoroughly for standard components, but there's nothing about integrating new UI elements with the authentication system," Andrea explained. "When I asked Mei, she said it's always been handled by Thomas as part of the testing process."

Jason nodded vigorously. "I ran into something similar with the testing framework. There's this unwritten handoff between development and testing that isn't captured anywhere."

Victor, having been quietly listening, spoke up. "We have a systematic gap in our documentation. We've documented individual components well, but not the integration points between them."

Marcia felt a chill of recognition. He was absolutely right. Their documentation had been created component by component, with each person documenting their own area of responsibility. The spaces between - the critical handoffs and integration points - had fallen through the cracks.

"That's a significant insight," she said, moving to the whiteboard. "Let's map these gaps while we're discovering them."

The next fifteen minutes was spent identifying integration points that lacked proper documentation: how the UI connected to the authentication system, how the reporting module interfaced with data sources, how automated testing covered cross-component functions.

The resulting diagram revealed a clear pattern - their knowledge management had a blind spot around the boundaries between systems.

"This isn't just a documentation issue," Marcia realised. "It reflects how we've been working. We've gotten better at collaboration, but we still think in terms of individual components rather than the system as a whole."

"A structural limitation of our team organisation," Victor observed. "Expertise and responsibility remain siloed despite our skills matrix improvements."

James appeared in the doorway, having overheard the conversation. "You've discovered what I call the 'white space problem' - the gaps between clearly defined responsibilities where critical integration happens."

The team looked up, surprised by his entrance but grateful for the perspective.

"Exactly," Marcia agreed. "Our documentation reflects our work structure - strong within domains but weak at the boundaries."

James nodded. "Most teams never identify this pattern, even when it causes repeated problems. The fact that you're recognising it explicitly is significant."

With this new awareness, they reorganised their approach to the remaining integration work. Instead of dividing tasks strictly by component, they created small cross-functional pairs specifically responsible for integration points.

Andrea and Jason teamed up to address the UI-authentication connection. Victor took on the reporting-data interface, with remote guidance from Mei when needed.

"Let's document these integration points as we solve them," Marcia suggested. "Not just the technical solutions, but the process - how these handoffs should work in the future."

By midday, a new section had appeared on their wiki titled "Integration Patterns," capturing both technical approaches and process handoffs at system boundaries.

Elizabeth called for her daily update, and Marcia shared their discovery about the documentation gaps.

"That's a valuable insight," Elizabeth said. "It's not just relevant to your team - it's a pattern I've seen across multiple projects."

✧ ✧ ✧

After lunch, a new challenge emerged. The latest build failed in a way no one had seen before. The error logs pointed to a configuration issue in the development environment - precisely the kind of problem Dmitri would typically handle.

"His environment documentation is thorough," Victor said, pulling up the relevant wiki page. "But it doesn't cover this specific error scenario."

Jason sighed. "Another gap at the boundaries - this time between the development environment and the build system."

They spent an hour trying various approaches based on Dmitri's documentation, but the error persisted. Finally, Marcia made a decision.

"I think we need to reach out to Dmitri, even though he's still sick. This is a critical blocker that could derail Friday's demonstration."

She sent a carefully worded message, explaining exactly what they needed and why it was critical. To everyone's surprise, Dmitri responded within minutes, not with text but with a screen recording. Despite being obviously ill, he had dragged himself to his home computer and created a ten-minute video walking through the exact steps needed to resolve the environment configuration issue.

"This is above and beyond," Marcia said as they watched the video together. "And exactly the kind of tacit knowledge that's hardest to document in advance."

The video unblocked their progress, allowing the integration to proceed. More importantly, Jason immediately added the solution to their wiki, ensuring they wouldn't face the same problem again.

By late afternoon, they had overcome most of the critical integration challenges. The system was coming together, though more slowly than originally planned.

During their end-of-day check-in, the team reflected on what they were learning through this crisis.

"We need to rethink how we structure our documentation," Andrea suggested. "Maybe organise it around user journeys and data flows that cross component boundaries, not just individual modules."

"And incorporate more visual representations of integration points," Jason added. "Text descriptions aren't always sufficient for complex interactions."

Breaking his long period of quiet contemplation, Victor offered an insight that stopped everyone: "Perhaps we should reconsider our team structure as well. Our documentation gaps reflect our organisational boundaries. If we realigned around service flows rather than technical components, both our work and our documentation would naturally address integration points."

The suggestion hung in the air, a profound observation that went beyond their immediate documentation challenges to the fundamental structure of how they worked.

"That's something to consider for the longer term," Marcia acknowledged. "For now, let's focus on documenting what we're learning about these integration points so we're better prepared next time."

As they wrapped up the day, Marcia felt a complex mix of emotions. They were making progress despite significant obstacles, which was encouraging. But the crisis had revealed structural limitations in their approach that wouldn't be easily fixed.

She updated their project status report with both the progress made and the challenges identified. Transparency had become a core value, and she wouldn't sugar-coat the situation even as they worked to resolve it.

James arrived with his usual timing as she was finishing for the day. "How's it going?"

"We're making progress on the technical integration," Marcia replied. "But we've uncovered some fundamental gaps in how we structure our work and documentation. Victor made an insightful observation about reorganising around service flows rather than technical components."

James nodded thoughtfully. "That's advanced organisational thinking. Most teams never get there, even after years together. The fact that you're having these conversations after just a few months is remarkable."

"It feels like we're still playing catch-up for Friday," Marcia shared with a concerned look.

"You are," James agreed candidly. "But you're also building lasting capabilities through this crisis. The team that emerges from this week will be fundamentally stronger than the one that entered it."

As Marcia gathered her things to leave, she received a message from Thomas that he planned to return tomorrow, though for a shortened day. Mei also confirmed she would be working remotely for most of Thursday. Things were looking up, if only slightly.

The perfect storm was still testing them, but it was also teaching them. The process gaps revealed under pressure weren't failures but opportunities - painful but valuable insights that would make them more resilient in the future.

✧ ✧ ✧

Thursday morning brought a welcome sight. Thomas walked through the office door at 9 am, looking pale but determined. The team broke into spontaneous applause as he made his way to his desk.

"Don't get too excited," he cautioned with a weak smile. "I'm operating at about sixty percent capacity. But that's better than zero."

Marcia felt a wave of relief. With Thomas back and Mei working remotely, they had a fighting chance to complete the integration for tomorrow's demonstration. Only Dmitri remained completely absent, now on his fourth sick day.

"Let's make this stand-up quick," Marcia suggested as they gathered around the visual task board. "We have a lot to accomplish today."

Andrea updated her cards first. "UI integration is about eighty percent complete. The documentation gaps we identified yesterday are slowing things down, but having Mei available remotely has been a huge help."

Jason nodded. "Testing framework is functional but not comprehensive. With Thomas back, we should be able to close the critical gaps today."

"The reporting module remains problematic," Victor admitted, his typically confident tone slightly hesitant. "There are integration points with the data layer that weren't fully documented. I've made progress but can't guarantee full functionality by tomorrow."

Thomas, listening carefully despite his obvious fatigue, spoke up. "I think we need to make a strategic decision about scope. We can't deliver everything as originally planned."

Marcia appreciated his directness. "You're right. Let's identify the absolute must-haves for tomorrow's demonstration and focus exclusively on those."

Together, they spent the next fifteen minutes ruthlessly prioritising features, creating a minimum viable product that would demonstrate the core functionality without requiring every integration point to be perfect.

"This is still going to be tight," Marcia acknowledged as they concluded. "But it's achievable if we stay focused."

As the team wandered back to their workstations, Marcia noticed something remarkable happening. Without any explicit direction, they had naturally formed collaborative pairs - Thomas guiding Jason through the testing framework, Andrea video-calling with Mei to solve UI issues, Victor reaching out to Thomas for help with reporting module integration.

The boundaries between components that had created their documentation gaps were being bridged through direct collaboration. People weren't just working on their assigned tasks; they were actively seeking connections across the system.

Elizabeth called mid-morning for her daily update.

"We've made a strategic decision to focus on core functionality for tomorrow," Marcia explained, being transparent about their situation. "Some of the more advanced features will need to be deferred to the next release."

"That's a sensible approach," Elizabeth replied. "Reliability is more important than bells and whistles." She trusted Marcia was doing her best to get the best outcome and didn't press further.

After the call, Marcia worked her way around the team, removing obstacles and facilitating connections. She noticed Thomas looking increasingly drained as the morning progressed.

"You should consider heading home after lunch," she told him quietly. "You've already made a huge difference by being here, and you need to recover."

Thomas shook his head stubbornly. "I'll stay as long as I can. There are integration points that only I fully understand."

"Then let's document those explicitly while you're here," Marcia suggested. "That gives us the benefit of your knowledge even after you leave."

He nodded, accepting the compromise. For the next two hours, Thomas worked with Jason to document the critical integration patterns between the testing framework and other components, creating clarity where there had previously been gaps.

By lunchtime, the team was making steady progress, but Marcia could see the strain starting to show. Everyone had been working at maximum intensity for days, covering for absent colleagues while racing against the deadline.

"Take a real lunch break," she instructed everyone. "Thirty minutes minimum, away from your desks. We need clear heads for the afternoon push."

As they reluctantly stepped away from their workstations, Marcia took a moment to update their status on the visual board. The picture was mixed - good progress on critical components but significant risks remaining, especially in the reporting module integration.

James appeared at her side, observing the board silently for a moment.

"How are you holding up?" he asked, his question clearly directed at her personally rather than the team as a whole.

"Hanging in there," Marcia replied, suddenly aware of her own exhaustion. "It's been intense."

"Leadership is often tested most visibly during crises," James observed. "But the foundation for successfully navigating those crises is built during calmer times."

Marcia considered this. "The systems we built when things were stable are carrying us now."

James nodded. "Exactly. If you hadn't established clear goals, documented processes, and built a collaborative culture, this week would have been catastrophic rather than merely challenging."

After lunch, Thomas reluctantly agreed to go home, his energy visibly depleted. Before leaving, he spent twenty minutes with Victor, walking through the reporting module integration that had been causing so much trouble.

As Thomas was gathering his things, Andrea approached Marcia with an unexpected suggestion.

"What if we did a focused code review session? All of us looking at the reporting module integration together, rather than leaving Victor to struggle with it alone?"

Marcia immediately saw the value. "That's brilliant. It addresses exactly the integration gap we've been struggling with."

For the next hour, the remaining team members gathered around Victor's desk, conducting an impromptu code review of the reporting module integration. Each person brought a different perspective - Andrea spotting UI connection issues, Jason identifying testing implications, Marcia focusing on overall user experience.

The collective intelligence of the team, focused on a single problem, proved remarkably effective. Connections that had been invisible to Victor working alone became obvious when viewed through multiple lenses.

"This is an approach we've been missing," Marcia realised. "Not just documenting individual components, but explicitly reviewing the integration points as a team."

By mid-afternoon, they had resolved the critical reporting module issues. The system wasn't perfect, but the core functionality required for tomorrow's demonstration was working reliably.

As they entered the final stretch, Marcia received an unexpected message from Dmitri: *Feeling slightly better. Can I help remotely with any critical issues?*

She quickly briefed him on their status, including the scope decisions they'd made. His response was immediate: *I'll review the build configuration to ensure stability for demo. No one should have to debug environment issues during presentation.*

Even from his sickbed, Dmitri was thinking about potential failure points that others might miss.

By 6 pm, they had assembled a working demonstration system with all the critical functionality in place. It wasn't everything they had originally planned, but it showcased the core capabilities reliably.

"Let's do one final run-through," Marcia suggested, gathering the team around Andrea's monitor.

Together, they walked through the demonstration script, testing each feature and identifying any remaining issues. The system held up, performing exactly as needed for tomorrow's presentation.

"We actually did it," Jason said, sounding slightly amazed. "Three days ago, I thought we were doomed."

"The documentation saved us," Andrea acknowledged. "Even with its gaps, it gave us a foundation to build on."

Victor, typically reserved with praise, added: "The team's response was... impressive. Systematic, adaptive, and ultimately effective."

As they wrapped up for the day, tired but satisfied, Marcia took a moment to appreciate what they had accomplished. Against significant odds, they had delivered a working system that met the core requirements.

"I'm incredibly proud of what we've achieved this week," she told the team. "Not just technically, but how we've worked together and adapted to challenges. This is what being a true team looks like."

Elizabeth's response to their final status update summed it up perfectly: "From what I've seen, you've turned a potential disaster into a testament to your team's resilience." Without telling Marcia, Elizabeth wrote an email to Robert expressing how she was impressed not just by what Marcia had delivered, but by how she delivered under extraordinary circumstances.

As Marcia shut down her computer, she reflected on the journey of the past week. The perfect storm had tested every aspect of their team's transformation - their processes, their documentation, their collaboration patterns, and their problem-solving approaches.

They had bent but not broken, adapting to each new challenge with increasing confidence. More importantly, they had identified structural improvements that would make them even stronger going forward.

Tomorrow's demonstration would be a milestone, but not an endpoint. The real achievement was the team itself - a group of talented individuals who had learned to function as something greater than the sum of their parts, even when operating at reduced capacity.

The perfect storm was passing, but it had left something valuable in its wake: a team that understood both its capabilities and its opportunities for growth, ready to tackle whatever challenges came next.

They had demonstrated sustainable excellence under pressure, and Marcia knew she no longer had to worry about Marcus and the infrastructure team.

Chapter 12
Full Circle

"Before we pop the champagne, let's take a moment to reflect," Marcia said, looking around the conference room at her team.

Friday afternoon had arrived, and with it, an overwhelming sense of relief. The demonstration for FreshWorks had gone remarkably well despite their perfect storm of absences. Not flawlessly - they'd encountered a minor UI glitch and had to skip one reporting feature - but the core functionality had performed exactly as needed, earning approving and thankful nods from Elizabeth.

Now, with Mei and Thomas back in the office and Dmitri joining remotely via Skype video, they had gathered for a retrospective on their challenging week.

"I want us to capture what we learned while it's fresh," Marcia continued. "The good, the bad, and everything in between."

She moved to the whiteboard and drew three simple columns: "What Worked Well," "What Could Be Better," and "Action Items."

"Let's start with what worked well," she suggested. "What saved us this week?"

Mei, still looking tired but much improved, spoke first. "The documentation was a lifesaver. Even with its gaps, it gave everyone enough foundation to pick up unfamiliar components."

Marcia nodded, writing "Documentation provided crucial knowledge transfer" on the board.

"The skills matrix was invaluable," Andrea added. "It helped us quickly identify who could cover which areas when people were out."

"Visual management kept us aligned," Jason said. "Without the task board, we would have lost track of dependencies and priorities during all the chaos."

Thomas, sipping tea to soothe his still-recovering throat, nodded. "And our daily stand-ups became even more important - they kept information flowing when we needed it most."

As the "What Worked Well" column filled, Marcia was struck by how their systematic improvements over the past months had created resilience they hadn't known they'd need. Each tool they'd implemented had contributed to their ability to weather the crisis.

"Now for the harder part," she prompted. "What could be better? Where did our systems fall short?"

Victor, always analytical, didn't hesitate. "Our documentation has a structural flaw. It's organised by component rather than by workflow, creating blind spots at integration points."

"Absolutely," Dmitri agreed from the video screen. "The handoffs between systems were our biggest vulnerability."

Marcia wrote "Documentation gaps at integration points" in the second column, followed by "Component-based vs. workflow-based structure."

"The skills coverage was uneven," Thomas noted. "Some areas had multiple people who could step in, while others had single points of failure."

"And our contingency planning was reactive, not proactive," Mei added. "We figured it out, but we didn't have a predetermined plan for covering key roles during absences."

The list in the second column grew, not with complaints but with thoughtful observations about systemic limitations. No one was pointing fingers or assigning blame - they were analysing patterns with a shared commitment to improvement.

When both columns contained robust lists, Marcia stepped back. "This is excellent insight. Now for the most important part - what specific actions can we take to strengthen our approach?"

"Restructure documentation around user journeys and data flows," Andrea suggested immediately. "That would naturally highlight integration points."

"Create explicit integration test plans that verify boundary functionality," Thomas added.

"Establish a more formal cross-training program to eliminate single points of failure," Mei proposed.

Victor, who had been quietly contemplative, spoke up. "I believe we should consider a more fundamental change to how we structure our work. Our current component-based organisation creates the very boundaries that caused problems this week."

"What do you have in mind?" Marcia asked, intrigued.

"A service-oriented structure," Victor explained, his typically reserved demeanour giving way to genuine enthusiasm. "Rather than organising primarily around technical components, we could align around service flows that naturally cross boundaries."

A thoughtful silence fell over the room as everyone considered this suggestion. It wasn't an incremental improvement but a fundamental rethinking of their approach.

"That's worth exploring," Marcia agreed, adding it to the action items. "It addresses the root cause rather than just the symptoms."

As they continued brainstorming actions, Marcia noticed something remarkable about the conversation. Four months ago, this team had struggled with basic coordination. Now they were having a sophisticated discussion about organisational design and systemic improvement.

"We've come a long way," she observed when they'd filled the action items column.

"It's night and day compared to when you first took over," Mei said with a smile. "Remember our first team meeting? When Victor and Dmitri wouldn't even make eye contact?"

Victor raised an eyebrow. "I recall being appropriately focused on technical concerns."

"That's Victor-speak for 'I was being difficult,'" Dmitri translated from the screen, prompting laughter from everyone - including Victor.

The easy camaraderie, even when discussing past tensions, highlighted another aspect of their transformation. They hadn't just improved processes and tools - they'd built relationships based on mutual respect and shared purpose.

"I'd like to implement these action items systematically," Marcia said, bringing them back to the task at hand. "Let's assign owners and timelines for each one."

With the same collaborative efficiency they'd shown all week, they divvied up responsibility for improvements. Victor would lead documentation restructuring. Thomas would develop integration test plans. Mei would establish cross-training protocols. Everyone had a role in strengthening their approach.

As they wrapped up, James appeared in the doorway. "Mind if I join you for a moment?"

"Perfect timing," Marcia said. "We've just finished our retrospective."

James studied the whiteboard with approval. "Impressive analysis. I particularly like that your action items address systemic changes, not just quick fixes."

"The team deserves all the credit," Marcia said. "They're not just solving today's problems - they're thinking about tomorrow's challenges."

"That's the mark of a mature team," James observed. "By the way, Robert asked me to convey his appreciation for the demonstration earlier. He mentioned that delivering successfully despite significant staffing challenges speaks volumes about your team's resilience."

The praise from Alpha's founder sent a ripple of pride through the room. They had earned this recognition the hard way - not through perfect execution but through perseverance and adaptation when faced with unexpected obstacles.

As the meeting concluded and team members began drifting back to their desks, Marcia stayed behind, studying the whiteboard filled with their collective insights. The retrospective had revealed both how far they'd come and how far they still had to go.

Their tools and processes had provided crucial support during the crisis, but also showed limitations they hadn't previously recognised. The challenge now was to strengthen those systems without losing their flexibility and collaborative spirit.

James lingered as well, seeming to follow her thoughts. "You know, the most valuable outcome of this week isn't the successful demonstration or even the specific improvements you've identified."

"What is it, then?" Marcia asked.

"The team has experienced firsthand why these systems matter," James replied. "Before, they were implementing tools because you suggested them. Now, they've felt the direct impact of those tools during a crisis. That creates a different level of commitment."

James's gaze lingered on the wall of action items. "Moments like this," he said, voice low, "remind me why I stayed in the game. Tools are temporary; the leaders you help shape - that's what lasts."

Marcia nodded slowly, recognising the truth in his observation. The perfect storm had turned their systematic approach from a theoretical good practice into a lived experience with tangible benefits.

As she gathered her notes, Marcia felt a deep sense of satisfaction mixed with renewed purpose. They were approaching the next phase with deeper understanding and stronger commitment, ready to build on the foundation they'd established together.

✧ ✧ ✧

"I think we need to make this official," Marcia said, setting a fresh coffee on Victor's desk.

It was Tuesday morning, the week after their successful demonstration - and crucially, the week after their revealing retrospective. The crisis had passed, with the team back at full strength and regular work resuming. But Marcia was determined not to lose the momentum they'd built.

Victor looked up from his monitor. "Make what official?"

"Our continuous improvement process." She pulled over a nearby chair. "Right now, we only conduct deep reviews like our retrospective when something goes wrong. What if we did them regularly, as a core part of how we work?"

Victor considered this, his expression thoughtful. "A systematic approach to identifying and implementing improvements would be logical. It would prevent regression to previous inefficient patterns."

"Exactly." Marcia smiled at his characteristically precise assessment. "I'm thinking monthly at first, then quarterly once we've addressed the most pressing issues."

"Similar to sprint retrospectives in agile methodologies, but with broader scope," Victor nodded. "I support this approach."

By lunchtime, Marcia had floated the idea to each team member, finding enthusiastic support. Even Dmitri, typically cautious about adding meetings, recognised the value of regular improvement cycles.

"Let's talk about this at tomorrow's team meeting," she suggested to each person. "Come prepared with thoughts on how we might structure it."

The next day, the team gathered in their usual conference room, but with a different energy than their crisis retrospective. This wasn't about recovering from challenges but about deliberately building on their progress.

"Last week we conducted a retrospective out of necessity," Marcia began. "It gave us valuable insights that are already improving our work. But why wait for the next crisis to get smarter?"

Mei nodded enthusiastically. "Regular review cycles would help us catch issues before they become problems."

"And give us space to think strategically, not just reactively," Thomas added.

"I've been researching different approaches," Andrea said, surprising Marcia with her initiative. "There are some interesting frameworks beyond basic retrospectives - systems thinking exercises, value stream mapping, even team performance metrics we could track over time."

"I'd like to propose a balanced approach," Victor said, pulling out a neatly organised document. "Monthly operational improvements focusing on immediate workflow enhancements, combined with quarterly strategic reviews addressing larger structural opportunities."

Marcia tried not to show her surprise at how thoroughly everyone had considered the idea. They weren't just agreeing - they were actively building on her initial concept with their own research and thoughts.

"This is fantastic input," she said. "Let's design something that works specifically for us."

What followed was one of the most engaging discussions they'd had as a team. They debated formats, cadences, and measurement approaches. They considered how to balance short-term fixes with long-term improvements. They even discussed rotating facilitation to ensure diverse perspectives.

"I think we're converging on a model," Marcia observed after nearly an hour of productive conversation. She moved to the whiteboard and sketched what they'd discussed:

1. Monthly Continuous Improvement Sessions (2 hours)
   o Focus: Operational enhancements and process refinements
   o Structure: Data review, issue identification, solution development
   o Outcomes: 3-5 specific improvements with owners and timelines
2. Quarterly Strategic Reviews (Half-day)
   o Focus: Structural improvements and capability development
   o Structure: Systems analysis, capability assessment, roadmap alignment
   o Outcomes: 1-2 major initiatives with implementation plans

3. Measurement & Tracking
   o Improvement Backlog: Prioritised list of enhancement opportunities
   o Impact Metrics: Quantifiable benefits from implemented changes
   o Visual Dashboard: Progress tracking visible to the entire team

"This looks right," Dmitri said, studying the whiteboard. "Structured yet flexible."

"And I like that we're focusing on outcomes, not just discussions," Thomas added.

As they finalised the details, Marcia felt a growing sense of pride. This wasn't her improvement process - it was theirs, shaped by their collective insights and experiences.

"We should document this," Mei suggested. "Make it part of our team wiki."

"I'd be happy to draft that," Andrea offered. "I can pull from the different frameworks I researched and customise it to our approach."

"And I can create the measurement dashboard," Jason added, already sketching ideas on his tablet.

By the end of the meeting, they had a clear plan for implementing continuous improvement as a formal part of their team operating model. What had begun as Marcia's suggestion had evolved into a collaborative creation reflecting everyone's contributions.

"Let's schedule our first session for next week," Marcia suggested. "That gives us time to gather data and prepare properly."

As the team returned to their tasks, James appeared in the doorway. He'd developed an uncanny ability to show up just as significant team moments concluded.

"Overheard bits of your discussion," he said. "Continuous improvement process?"

"The team's designed an impressive approach," Marcia confirmed, showing him the whiteboard. "Monthly operational reviews and quarterly strategic assessments, with clear outcomes and tracking metrics."

James studied the design with obvious approval. "This is sophisticated work. Most teams never progress beyond ad hoc improvements."

"It's entirely their creation," Marcia said. "I suggested regular reviews, but they built this comprehensive framework themselves."

James nodded, a hint of pride in his eyes. "That's the real marker of success. They're not just following your lead anymore - they're thinking like owners."

He paused, thoughtful. "As they continue to grow into a self-managing team, you might find your role shifts too - from leading to coaching."

✧ ✧ ✧

The following week, they held their first official Continuous Improvement Session. Unlike previous retrospectives focused on specific issues, this session took a systematic approach to analysing their overall workflow.

Victor had volunteered to facilitate, drawn to the structured data analysis portion. He arrived with color-coded printouts and a meticulously prepared agenda that outlined precisely how many minutes each segment should take.

"I've created a framework for our analysis," he explained, distributing his materials with characteristic precision. "We'll examine workflow efficiency using quantitative metrics first, then identify statistically significant bottlenecks."

Ten minutes in, Marcia noticed Victor's growing discomfort as the conversation naturally drifted from his planned structure. His shoulders tensed as Mei raised points that weren't on his agenda, and he repeatedly checked his watch when discussions extended beyond their allocated timeframes.

"Perhaps we should move to the testing process analysis now," he suggested, a slight edge in his voice as he attempted to redirect the conversation back to his prepared path.

Recognising his increasing anxiety, Marcia gently stepped in. "Victor has prepared excellent data analysis for us. Let's focus on that for the next segment, then we can open up for broader discussion afterward."

Victor shot her a grateful look as the team returned to his structured approach, revealing valuable insights about bottlenecks in their testing process. Thomas then naturally took the lead on problem-solving around those bottlenecks, building on Victor's analysis while allowing more free-flowing conversation.

Jason demonstrated the dashboard he'd created for tracking implementation and measuring impact, which gave Victor an opportunity to contribute specific technical improvements without the pressure of facilitation.

The session wasn't perfect - they'd spent too long on data review and rushed the solution development - but the foundation was solid. More importantly, they'd found a natural rhythm that leveraged everyone's strengths: Victor's analytical rigor, Thomas's practical problem-solving, Jason's visualisation skills, and Mei's people-focused insights.

They ended with clear actions and a shared commitment to making tangible improvements before their next session.

"Good first session," Marcia told the team as they wrapped up. "We'll refine the format as we go."

Victor approached her afterward. "Thank you for the assistance," he said quietly. "The unstructured discussion was... challenging to manage."

"That's why this works," Marcia replied with a smile. "You excel at the data analysis that grounds our decisions in facts. Others fill different roles. Together, we create something stronger than any one approach."

Victor considered this, then nodded. "A system of complementary components. Logical."

✧ ✧ ✧

Over the following weeks, the impact of the teams continuous improvement process became increasingly visible. Small enhancements accumulated into noticeable efficiency gains. Testing bottlenecks that had plagued them for months were systematically addressed. Documentation improved based on insights from their crisis experience.

More subtly, the team's mindset shifted. Problems weren't just irritations to work around - they were opportunities to improve the system. When Andrea encountered an issue with the development environment, her first response wasn't frustration but analysis: What systemic factor caused this? How could they prevent it from happening again?

By their third monthly session, the process had hit its stride. Dmitri facilitated this time, bringing his characteristic precision to the data review while encouraging creative problem-solving. They identified four specific improvements and reviewed progress on previous initiatives, celebrating measurable gains in development cycle time and defect reduction.

"We're getting good at this," Mei observed as they wrapped up.

"It's becoming part of how we work," Marcia agreed. "Not a separate activity but an integrated aspect of our approach."

Later that afternoon, Robert Miller himself stopped by the Enterprise Solutions area - a rare occurrence that immediately caught everyone's attention.

"James tells me you've implemented a systematic continuous improvement process," he said, getting straight to the point as usual. "I'd like to learn more about your approach."

As the team explained their framework, Robert listened with characteristic attentiveness, occasionally asking incisive questions about measurement methods and implementation tracking.

"This is exactly the kind of disciplined improvement cycle we need across Alpha," he said when they'd finished. "Effective without being bureaucratic, data-driven without losing practicality."

He turned to Marcia. "Would your team be willing to present this framework at our leadership offsite next month? I want all our team leaders to see what's possible."

"We'd be honoured," Marcia replied, glancing around to see nods of agreement from the team.

After Robert left, a moment of quiet pride settled over the group. Their journey had come full circle - from a struggling team adopting basic tools to a model that others would learn from.

Jason let out a low whistle. "First he says we should be a model team... now we're presenting at the leadership offsite?"

"That's right," Marcia confirmed, smiling. "And it's well-deserved recognition for what you've built."

As she returned to her desk, Marcia reflected on the significance of this moment. The continuous improvement process wasn't just another tool in their kit - it was the mechanism that would sustain and enhance all their other systems over time.

They had created not just a better way of working, but a way of continually getting better.

The perfect storm had tested their resilience. That evening, updating her leadership journal, Marcia wrote:

The mark of a truly effective team isn't just what they can achieve today, but how systematically they improve for tomorrow. We've crossed that threshold - from executing tasks to evolving capabilities, from following processes to enhancing systems.

✧ ✧ ✧

The knock at Marcia's cubicle was tentative, almost hesitant. She looked up to see Ryan Davis standing there, a mix of determination and anxiety on his face.

"Do you have a minute?" he asked.

"For you? Always," Marcia replied, gesturing to the chair across from her desk. "How's your first week going?"

Ryan had just been promoted to lead the Customer Experience team - a group with challenges reminiscent of what the Enterprise Solutions team had faced six months earlier. Talented individuals working in silos, inconsistent processes, and mounting pressure from stakeholders. A familiar story.

"Honestly? I'm overwhelmed," Ryan admitted as he sat down, interlocking his hands and rocking slightly. "The team is fragmented, nobody seems to know what the priorities are, and I've got three different directors asking for status updates in three different formats."

Marcia nodded sympathetically. "Sounds familiar."

"That's why I'm here," Ryan said. "Everyone keeps telling me how you transformed your team. I was hoping you might have some advice."

Marcia smiled. In the eight months since she'd reluctantly taken on leadership of Enterprise Solutions, her team had become something of a legend at Alpha. Their systems, their collaboration, their continuous improvement approach - all had become examples that other teams sought to emulate.

"I'm happy to help," she said. "But first, tell me what you see as your biggest challenges."

For the next ten minutes, Ryan described a situation that could have been Enterprise Solutions' twin - unclear goals, inconsistent processes, knowledge silos, and low visibility into actual progress.

"The frustrating part is that they're all smart, capable people," he concluded. "But somehow together they're less than the sum of their parts."

"That's exactly where we started," Marcia said. "A collection of talented individuals rather than a true team."

She stood and moved to her whiteboard, uncapping a marker. "If I were to distil what worked for us into a simple framework, it would look something like this."

She drew a pyramid with four levels.

"Start with alignment," she explained, labelling the foundation layer. "Team goals, shared priorities, clear direction. Without this, nothing else matters."

She added the second layer. "Then build visibility - make work transparent, manage tasks visually, communicate status consistently. This creates trust and surfaces issues early."

The third layer followed. "Next comes capability development - understand who can do what, share knowledge systematically, close skill gaps deliberately."

She capped the pyramid with the final layer. "And at the top, continuous improvement - regular review cycles, measured enhancements, evolving systems."

Ryan studied the diagram intently. "That makes logical sense. But where do I actually start? Monday morning, I'll walk in and face the same chaos."

Marcia smiled at the familiar feeling. "Monday morning, you do exactly one thing - begin understanding what matters most to your team."

She erased the pyramid and drew a simpler diagram with three overlapping circles.

"This was the most important insight for me," she said. "A team functions at its best when three elements align: what the business needs, what customers value, and what motivates your team members."

She tapped the center where all three circles overlapped. "Find this intersection, and you'll discover your true team goals."

"So I should just ask them what they care about?" Ryan seemed sceptical.

"Not quite," Marcia replied. "Structure the conversation. Ask specific questions about what success looks like from their perspective. What would make them proud of their work? What frustrates them most in the current approach? What do they think customers actually value?"

Ryan took notes as she explained her approach, asking thoughtful questions about facilitation techniques and how to handle potential resistance.

"The key is framing it as discovery, not criticism," Marcia emphasised. "You're not telling them what's wrong - you're helping them articulate what could be better."

"And after we establish goals?" Ryan asked.

"Then you make work visible," Marcia said, pulling out photos of their visual task board. "This was our second breakthrough. When everyone can see what's happening, who's doing what, and where the obstacles are, everything changes."

She walked Ryan through their journey - the skills matrix that mapped capabilities, the documentation system that preserved knowledge, the roadmap that connected daily work to strategic objectives, and finally, the continuous improvement process that kept them evolving.

"It's a lot to take in," Ryan admitted, looking slightly overwhelmed again.

"You don't do it all at once," Marcia reassured him. "Start with team goals, then task visibility. Build from there, with the team's input at every step."

"How long did this take for your team?"

"About two months for the foundational elements," Marcia replied. "But you'll see positive changes much sooner than that. The first team goals workshop will already shift the dynamic."

Ryan nodded, a new determination in his expression. "This helps enormously. Thank you."

As he stood to leave, Marcia had a thought. "Would it help if I facilitated your first team goals session? Sometimes having an outside perspective makes it easier."

Ryan's relief was visible. "That would be amazing - if you can spare the time."

"Consider it done," Marcia said. "And afterward, I'm happy to keep providing guidance as you build your approach."

After Ryan left, Marcia leaned back in her chair, feeling a sense of completion. She remembered how James had mentored her through those challenging early days, offering frameworks and insights when she needed them most.

Now she was paying that forward, helping another leader navigate the same difficult transition from technical contributor to team builder.

James appeared in her doorway, as if summoned by her thoughts. "Was that Ryan Davis I saw leaving?"

"It was," Marcia confirmed. "He's looking for guidance on transforming his team."

"And you're the natural person to provide it," James observed. "That's why I asked him to come and see you. The student becomes the teacher."

"I'm just sharing what worked for us," Marcia said modestly.

"That's how organisational knowledge grows," James replied. "Individual learning becomes team practice, which becomes shared wisdom."

The following week, Marcia facilitated Ryan's first team goals workshop. Watching the Customer Experience team struggle with the same questions hers had faced months earlier, she recognised both the challenges and the potential.

"They're exactly where we were," she told James later, describing the session. "Talented people who don't yet see how they could be stronger together."

"Will they succeed?" James asked pragmatically.

"I think they will," Marcia replied. "Ryan has the right mindset - curious, systematic, and focused on enabling rather than directing. And they have one advantage we didn't."

"What's that?"

"A working example they can observe," Marcia said. "Our team has shown what's possible, created templates they can adapt, and proven that the approach delivers results."

Over the following weeks, Marcia met regularly with Ryan, providing guidance as he implemented each element of the framework. She shared templates, facilitated key sessions, and offered perspective when he encountered obstacles.

The parallels to her own journey were striking - the initial resistance from some team members, the breakthrough moments when systems began to connect, the gradual shift from fragmentation to cohesion.

Two months later, Ryan stopped by with an update and a gift - a framed photo of his team's newly established visual task board.

"We're making real progress," he reported proudly. "Goals are clear, work is visible, and we're starting to document our knowledge. The team is actually excited about what we're building together."

"That's fantastic," Marcia said, genuinely pleased by his progress.

"I couldn't have done it without your guidance," Ryan said. "Knowing there was a path - that someone had successfully navigated these challenges before - made all the difference."

After he left, Marcia hung the framed photo on her wall, next to the team goals poster from their own journey. It was a tangible reminder that her impact extended beyond her immediate work.

✧ ✧ ✧

The late afternoon sun slanted through the windows of Alpha Consulting's conference room as Marcia gathered her notes. The quarterly business review had just concluded, and for once, the Enterprise Solutions team's presentation had generated minimal questions. Their methodical approach, clear metrics, and transparent reporting had become so reliable that executives now used them as a benchmark for other teams.

"That went well," Mei said, helping collect the printed handouts they'd distributed.

"Almost too well," Marcia replied with a smile. "I was prepared for at least some challenging questions."

"When you consistently deliver and communicate effectively, you earn the luxury of boring meetings," James observed, shutting down his laptop.

As they walked back to their team area, Marcia felt a familiar blend of pride and reflection. In the ten months since she'd reluctantly stepped into leadership, their transformation had exceeded her wildest expectations. The fractured group she'd inherited had become a true team - aligned in purpose, systematic in approach, and continuously improving.

Back at her cubicle, Marcia found an email notification blinking on her laptop screen. She clicked on the Outlook icon, watching as dozens of unread messages populated her inbox. Among the flood of status updates and meeting invitations, a message from Robert Miller requesting a private meeting the following morning stood out. Despite their increasingly positive relationship, a summons from Alpha's founder still triggered a flutter of anxiety.

"Everything okay?" James asked, noticing her expression as he passed by.

"Robert wants to meet tomorrow morning. No agenda specified."

James smiled enigmatically. "I might know what that's about."

"Care to share?" Marcia asked.

"I think he should tell you himself," James replied. "But I wouldn't worry."

The next morning, Marcia arrived at Robert's office precisely on time, notebook in hand rather than a tablet, despite being a technology consulting firm. His assistant waved her directly in.

"Marcia, thank you for coming," Robert greeted her, gesturing to the chair across from his desk. The founder looked characteristically focused, but there was a warmth in his expression that hadn't been there during their early interactions.

"I'll get straight to the point," he continued. "Your leadership of the Enterprise Solutions team over the past ten months has been exemplary. Further, the leadership team has been impressed with how you presented at the offsite, and how you've helped Ryan Davis implement effective team practices.

What you've built is becoming a model for other teams across Alpha."

"Thank you," Marcia replied, genuinely appreciative but still uncertain where this was heading.

"We're growing rapidly," Robert continued. "We've nearly hit one hundred employees here in Seattle, and we're looking at opening our first satellite office in San Francisco next quarter."

Marcia nodded. The company's expansion had been a frequent topic at leadership meetings.

"With this growth comes new opportunities," Robert said, leaning forward. "I'd like to establish a formal 'Team Excellence' program with you as the lead. Your team would continue its current responsibilities while serving as a centre of excellence for these practices. I'd like to offer you a promotion to Practice Lead - Team Excellence, effective next month."

Marcia blinked in surprise. "That's... that's wonderful. Thank you."

"You've earned it," Robert said simply. "The role will involve leading more complex projects and occasionally mentoring other team leaders who are implementing your methodologies."

"What about my current team?" Marcia asked, immediately thinking of the group she'd helped transform.

"That's where I'd like your input," Robert replied. "You've built a team that doesn't depend solely on you anymore. They have the systems, the clarity, and the collaborative culture to continue excelling with a new leader at the helm."

The observation struck Marcia deeply. Robert was right - she'd worked hard to create a team that functioned as a system rather than relying on any individual, including herself. Their processes, documentation, and continuous improvement mechanisms ensured they could maintain momentum through transitions.

"I'd like you to recommend your successor," Robert continued. "Someone who understands the systems you've built and can continue evolving them rather than replacing them with their own approach."

Marcia nodded, already considering possibilities. "When would this transition happen?"

"We're looking at four weeks from now," Robert replied. "That gives you time to prepare your team for the change and begin transition planning."

As Marcia left Robert's office, she felt a complex mix of emotions - excitement about the new challenge, pride in the recognition, but also a surprising pang at the thought of stepping away from the team she'd helped transform.

James was waiting near her desk, leaning against the beige cubicle wall. "From your expression, I'm guessing he told you about the promotion."

"He did," Marcia confirmed. "How long have you known?"

"Since the executive committee made the decision last week," James admitted. "I advocated for you."

"Thank you for your confidence," Marcia said sincerely. "But I'll miss working with the team we've built."

"That's natural," James acknowledged. "But remember - the greatest test of a leader isn't what happens when they're present, but what continues when they're not."

That afternoon, Marcia called a special team meeting. Looking around at the assembled faces - Victor's analytical focus, Mei's empathetic attention, Thomas's quiet reliability, Dmitri's systematic thinking, Andrea's fresh perspective, Jason's creative energy - she felt a surge of affection for the group they'd become. Not everyone could attend due to conflicting meetings, but Marcia felt it important for her to share the news directly.

"I have some news to share," she began. "Robert Miller has offered me a promotion to Practice Lead - Team Excellence starting next month."

A moment of surprised silence was followed by a chorus of congratulations, though she noticed the flicker of concern beneath their supportive words.

"This means I'll be transitioning to a new role," Marcia continued, watching their expressions carefully. "And someone else will step in to lead this team."

"Who?" Thomas asked the question on everyone's mind.

"That's not decided yet," Marcia replied. "Robert has asked for my recommendation, and I'll be thinking carefully about that over the next few days."

"What matters most in your decision?" Mei asked, closing a tab she had open on her laptop.

Marcia considered the question carefully. "Someone who understands and values the systems we've built together. Who will preserve what works while continuing to evolve our approach. Who sees their role as enabling your collective excellence rather than directing your individual actions."

The team nodded thoughtfully.

"I have four weeks before the transition," Marcia added. "During that time, I want to ensure everything we've built together is rock-solid - our goals framework, visual management system, documentation, continuous improvement process. We'll create a comprehensive transition plan to make this change as smooth as possible."

The conversation that followed was both practical and poignant - questions about timing, suggestions for strengthening documentation, concerns about maintaining momentum. Throughout it all, Marcia noticed how the team approached the news: not with resistance or anxiety, but with the same systematic problem-solving they brought to technical challenges.

"We should document the leadership principles that have worked well," Victor suggested. "Not as rigid rules, but as guidance for your successor."

"And update our roadmap to show key decision points over the next six months," Dmitri added.

After the meeting, Marcia stayed behind in the conference room, reflecting on the journey they'd taken together. From fragmented individuals to cohesive team. From reactive firefighting to proactive improvement. From struggling project to model for the organisation.

James joined her, leaning against the doorframe. "How did they take it?"

"They took it really well," Marcia reflected. "They immediately started planning how to make the transition successful."

"You've taught them well," James observed. "They're approaching this change the same way they approach everything else - systematically, collaboratively, focused on what matters."

"I'm going to miss them," Marcia said quietly.

"Of course you will," James acknowledged. "But you're not leaving them behind - you're taking everything you've learned together into your next challenge. And they'll carry those same lessons forward with your successor."

Over the following weeks, Marcia worked with the team to create a comprehensive transition plan. They documented leadership approaches, updated roadmaps, clarified decision frameworks, and strengthened communication protocols - printing binders of materials rather than relying solely on digital formats, knowing that tangible resources often proved more accessible in the daily bustle of work. It wasn't about creating rigid rules for her successor, but about preserving the systematic foundation they'd built together.

The question of who would take over remained open until the third week, when Marcia finally made her recommendation to Robert: Mei, whose combination of technical skill, emotional intelligence, and systematic thinking made her ideally suited to continue what they'd started.

Robert approved the selection immediately. "An excellent choice. She understands both the technical requirements and the human dynamics."

✧ ✧ ✧

On Marcia's final Friday with the team, they gathered for a special retrospective - not focused on recent work, but on their entire journey together. The familiar conference room had been transformed with printed charts showing their progress over the past months, visual evidence of their transformation.

"When I stepped into this role eleven months ago, I was reluctant and uncertain," Marcia shared openly. "I had technical skills but little leadership experience. What I discovered was that leadership isn't about having all the answers - it's about creating the conditions where a team can find answers together."

"You gave us structure when we needed it most," Thomas said quietly.

"But not rigid control," Victor added. "Systematic frameworks that enhanced rather than limited our capabilities."

"You showed us how to be more than the sum of our parts," Andrea observed.

After the formal retrospective, the team presented Marcia with a gift - a bound book containing printed copies of their team goals, samples from the skills matrix, process documentation, and continuous improvement framework, along with personal notes from each team member.

"So you never forget what we built together," Mei explained, her eyes bright with emotion.

Marcia ran her fingers over the cover, deeply touched by the gesture. "I couldn't forget if I tried. This experience has fundamentally changed how I approach work - and leadership."

As she packed up her cubicle later that afternoon, sorting through printed documents and the few personal items she'd accumulated, James stopped by one last time.

Marcia paused in her packing, holding a framed team photo. Six months ago, the thought of speaking to executives about leadership would have sent her into a spiral of preparation and anxiety. Now, she felt something different - not the absence of nervousness, but the presence of earned confidence.

"Ready for your next challenge?" James asked, leaning against the cubicle's divider with that familiar knowing smile.

"As ready as I'll ever be," Marcia smiled noting how different she felt since she last said that, carefully placing the photo into her cardboard box. She ran her finger along the frame, remembering the day it was taken - right after they'd successfully delivered the FreshWorks project against impossible odds. "Though I'm guessing Practice Lead comes with a whole new curriculum of leadership lessons."

"The best kind of lessons," James nodded. "The ones you don't see coming."

He stepped into her nearly-empty cubicle, surveying the bare walls where process maps and team charts had hung just hours before. "You know, the reluctant developer I practically forced into leadership last year wouldn't recognise the leader standing here today."

"She'd probably run the other direction," Marcia laughed.

"Maybe. But she didn't have what you have now - a proven approach to building effective teams that you can apply anywhere. That's the real promotion."

James gestured toward the glass-walled conference room, where Marcia's team - Mei's team now - clustered around their visual board. Victor was pointing at something while Dmitri nodded thoughtfully. Andrea was sketching rapidly on a sticky note as Thomas leaned in to see. The familiar choreography of a team that knew how to move together.

"That's the true measure of leadership success," James said softly. "Not what you accomplish yourself, but what you enable others to accomplish together."

Marcia felt her throat tighten unexpectedly. Pride in what they'd accomplished together. Confidence in Mei's readiness to lead. Excitement about helping other teams transform. And yes, a bittersweet ache that came with letting go of something precious.

But watching them work - the visual board they'd designed together, the documentation system that captured their collective wisdom, the continuous improvement cycle that never stopped evolving - she realised this wasn't really an ending.

Last year, she'd inherited a collection of talented individuals who couldn't function as a team. Today, she was leaving behind something far more valuable: a living system that would continue growing long after she'd gone. Team goals that provided direction. Skills matrices that matched talents to tasks. Visual management that created transparency. Documentation that preserved knowledge. Improvement cycles that prevented stagnation.

These weren't just tools they used - they were patterns of thinking, habits of collaboration, ways of working that had become part of their DNA.

And she would carry those same patterns into her next challenge, along with the most important lesson of all: leadership wasn't about having all the answers - it was about creating the conditions where teams could discover them together.

Marcia lifted her box of belongings, feeling the weight of the team's parting gift - a bound collection of their journey together - along with her young thriving jade plant balanced on top. She took one final look at the space that had witnessed her transformation from reluctant team leader to confident practice lead.

Then she stepped forward into whatever came next, not as someone pushed into leadership, but as someone who had discovered that building bridges between talented people was the most challenging code she'd ever written - and the most rewarding program she'd ever run.

Epilogue

- Six Months Later -

The whiteboard in Marcia's office still bore the faint shadows of a dozen planning diagrams, hastily erased in meetings that never seemed to end. She smiled at the ghosts of arrows and boxes, then capped her marker and turned toward the younger woman standing nervously in the doorway.

"Come in, Lila," Marcia said. "Grab a chair. First week as team lead - how's it treating you?"

Lila, a senior developer who'd just been promoted, sank into the seat with a sigh. "Honestly? It feels like everyone's waiting for me to screw up. Half the team's older than me, and Victor keeps giving me that raised eyebrow look. I'm trying to act confident, but inside I feel like a fraud."

Marcia leaned forward, hands folded on the desk. The words were so familiar it was almost uncanny - like hearing her own thoughts from eighteen months ago. "You're not a fraud. You're a beginner at a new job. That's different."

Lila gave a sceptical smile. "Easy for you to say. You make it look effortless."

Marcia laughed. "Effortless? You didn't see me hiding in the parking garage on my first week, wondering if I should quit."

That got Lila's full attention. "You? Quit?"

"I was ready to," Marcia admitted. "People having faith in me helped until I believed in myself more."

She reached into her bag and pulled out the worn spiral notebook. "I started keeping a log when I first became a team lead."

Its cover was faded; the edges of the pages feathered with ink and sticky notes. "Every hard moment went in here. Not always solutions, sometimes just questions. Like: What does the team really need from me today? What's the one thing only I can do right now?"

She slid the notebook across the desk. "Read a page."

Lila hesitated, then flipped to a section marked with a crooked tab. Her eyes moved down the scrawled handwriting:

When in doubt, convene the team. People fear the unknown more than bad news.

She looked up. "That's... good."

Marcia nodded. "It worked. Not every time, but often enough. And you'll start building your own list soon. Keep a log. Write down what scares you, what surprises you, what works. It's the best debugging tool for leadership."

Lila closed the notebook gently and pushed it back across the desk. "Thanks. That makes it feel... survivable."

"It is," Marcia said. She leaned back, letting herself enjoy the moment. Lila was still pale with nerves, but her shoulders had relaxed a little. "One day you'll be the one handing advice to the next new lead. That's how this works."

From the hallway came the muffled buzz of voices and the squeak of rolling chairs. Another team was waiting for Marcia to join their design session - cross-department, high stakes, the kind of meeting that six months ago she would have dreaded.

Now, she felt only the quiet hum of readiness.

"Come on," she said, standing. "You're with me this afternoon. It's a joint workshop with product, and I want you in the room. Not as an observer - as a contributor."

Lila's eyes widened. "Me? Already?"

"Especially you. You'll learn more in an hour of messy discussion than in a week of clean plans. Besides," Marcia tapped the notebook before tucking it back into her bag. "I have a feeling you'll want to write a few things down afterward."

They stepped into the corridor together, the office buzzing with the friction of deadlines and half-formed ideas. Marcia glanced at the glass-walled conference room where her team was already gathering, and for a moment she saw herself reflected - smaller, less certain, standing in this same hallway months ago.

She wasn't that person anymore.

And maybe, just maybe, she could help someone else make the same leap.

Marcia opened the door and held it for Lila. "Welcome to leadership. Let's get to work."

Conclusion

Leadership doesn't begin with confidence. It begins with curiosity - about your people, your environment, and yourself.

Marcia's journey from overwhelmed technician to capable team leader wasn't about having all the answers. It was about learning how to observe, how to listen, and how to create the conditions for her team to thrive. Along the way, she discovered that real leadership is less about control and more about building systems, rhythms, and relationships that work together.

If you've seen parts of yourself in Marcia, that's no accident. Whether you're leading for the first time or navigating a new team dynamic, the challenges she faced - misalignment, missed expectations, broken trust - are common across industries. So are the solutions: clear goals, honest conversations, thoughtful delegation, and a focus on both outcomes and people.

As you go forward, consider:

- What systems are you building?
- Where do you need more clarity, or more trust?
- What would your team build, if you stepped back just a little - and asked them how they'd do it?

You now have the tools - a framework, a mindset, and a model. More importantly, you know that great leadership isn't about perfection. It's about progress, reflection, and showing up to do the real work - one conversation at a time.

Thank you for reading. Keep building.

Ready to lead the way for someone else?

If *Team Leaders Toolbox* helped you navigate your own leadership journey, sharing a quick review can do more than you think. It helps others decide to step forward - and gives this book a chance to reach the next emerging leader who needs it.

To leave a review

▦ *Scan the QR code on this page*

💬 *Or go to your Amazon Orders → find this book →*
"Write a Product Review"

Your insights could be the nudge
that builds someone else's confidence.

With gratitude,
Stephen J. McIntyre

About the Author

Stephen J. McIntyre is an author, startup entrepreneur, and delivery assurance practice lead at New Zealand's largest homegrown professional services and technology company. With over 30 years of leadership experience across tech startups, enterprise programs, and property development, Stephen is known for bringing calm thinking, structured problem-solving, and heart-led leadership into fast-moving environments.

He began writing *Team Leaders Toolbox*, driven by a desire to help first-time leaders navigate the shift from expert to team builder. After years of rewrites, experiments, and learning from real-world projects, Stephen discovered that the best way to teach leadership was through story. The result is this business parable - crafted to be engaging, relatable, and full of moments you'll recall when it matters most.

Stephen's leadership training began in the NZ Territorial Forces (part-time Army), and he continues to grow leaders today as a professional coach and active Toastmasters member. He reads over 50 books a year across leadership, psychology, and strategy - blending insights from the page with lessons from the field.

He lives in Auckland with his wife and daughter, and believes great leadership is less about having all the answers - and more about building teams that find them together.

Resources

Bring the story to life with editable templates and practical tools inspired by *Team Leaders Toolbox*. These resources are designed to help you apply what Marcia used: right in your own team.

Team Leader Essentials Toolkit
- **The 4 Essential Tools**
  - Team Goals Examples (from real teams)
  - Skills Matrix Template
  - Roadmap Template
  - Resource Allocation Plan Template
- **"What's On This Week" Email Examples** - Structure your weekly team email like Marcia's: updates, priorities, and expectations at a glance
- **Task Board Examples** - Options for physical walls, whiteboards, or digital tools

Communication & Trust-Building Tools
- **30 Icebreakers & Connection Prompts** - For team building, retrospectives, or one-on-one meetings
- **One-on-one, Desk Visit, and Monthly Review Questions** - For affirming, redirecting, and coaching team members
- **Meeting Facilitation Cheat Sheet** - For running successful meetings
- **Team Building – The Drawing Game** - To help teams understand communication needs when the team composition changes

For New or Aspiring Leaders
- **First 90 Days Planning Canvas** - Clarify your early goals, relationships, and team strategy
- **Recommended Reading List** - Handpicked list of beginner-friendly books and articles
- **Team Charter Template** - Co-create team norms, values, and working agreements

Ongoing Growth & Practice
- **Printable Poster: The 4 Tools at a Glance**
- **Journal Reflection Prompts** - For personal leadership growth and decision clarity
- **Monthly Manager's Letter** (via email) - Actionable tips, reader stories, and exclusive previews from future books

Extras & Behind-the-Scenes
- **Team Rituals That Worked** - Real-world rituals from readers and leaders who used the book
- **Sneak Peek:** *The 7 Hidden Powers of Effective Managers* - Discover what happens next in Marcia's journey
- **Upcoming Titles** - Early access to *Delivery Mindset* and *Leading Change*

☞ Download at: https://echostorymedia.com/toolbox
(Or scan the QR code below)

Recommended Reading

Coming soon in the *Lead With Confidence* series:

The 7 Hidden Powers of Effective Managers
Delivery Mindset
Leading Change
Lessons Learned

Recommended books to deepen your leadership journey beyond *Team Leaders Toolbox*:

Atomic Habits by James Clear
Dare to Lead by Brené Brown
Drive by Daniel H. Pink
Radical Candor by Kim Scott
Start with Why by Simon Sinek
The Checklist Manifesto by Atul Gawande
The Five Dysfunctions of a Team by Patrick Lencioni
The Hard Thing About Hard Things by Ben Horowitz
The Lean Startup by Eric Ries
They Ask, You Answer by Marcus Sheridan

Referenced Frameworks & Concepts

The story incorporates several well-established workplace and leadership approaches, which are acknowledged here for context and clarity:

Agile Standups & Task Boards - widely used practices from agile project management.

Delegation Frameworks - widely used approaches for clarifying ownership and decision rights. Marcia demonstrates this by handing responsibility to team members, asking them to draft frameworks or lead portions of meetings, and making ownership explicit.

Eisenhower Matrix - a 2x2 prioritisation framework (urgent/not-urgent vs. important/not-important). While not explicitly named, Marcia often applies similar logic, such as focusing on root-cause issues despite urgent demands and prioritising long-term capacity over short-term fixes.

Feedback Loops & Retrospectives - principles from agile and continuous improvement methodologies.

Growth Mindset - a concept introduced by Carol Dweck, describing the belief that abilities can be developed through effort, learning, and feedback. Marcia demonstrates this by modelling vulnerability, curiosity, and celebrating effort as well as results. She openly admits she doesn't have all the answers.

Kaizen / Continuous Improvement - a principle of making ongoing, incremental improvements rather than waiting for big changes. Marcia applies this by guiding the team through small process tweaks (stand-ups, task boards, skills matrix) that compound into major performance gains.

Situational Leadership - originally developed by Hersey & Blanchard. Marcia flexes between directive, coaching, supportive, and delegating styles depending on the individual and context.

Skills Matrix - a common tool for mapping team capability and identifying development opportunities.

SMART Goals - a structured goal-setting framework. Although not formally named, elements of this approach appear when the team defines priorities, clarifies success criteria, and discusses timelines and scope.

Systems Thinking - the practice of viewing teams, processes, and outcomes as interconnected elements rather than isolated tasks. This is highlighted in James's mentoring sessions with Marcia, where he frames problems in terms of task, process, and people interactions.

Psychological Safety - a concept popularised by Amy Edmondson in *The Fearless Organisation*, describing environments where individuals feel safe to take risks and be open. Marcia encourages honesty, treats mistakes as learning data, builds trust through consistency, and follows through on commitments.

Thanks & Acknowledgements

Special thanks to the leaders, teams, mentors, and clients - past and present - whose real-world challenges helped shape this story.